PLAYBACK

Ronald Hayman

PLAYBACK

DAVIS-POYNTER

First published in 1973 by
Davis-Poynter Limited
20 Garrick Street, London WC2F 9BJ

Copyright © 1973 by Ronald Hayman

ISBN 0 7067 0076 7

PRINTED IN GREAT BRITAIN BY
BRISTOL TYPESETTING CO. LTD.
BARTON MANOR - ST. PHILIPS
BRISTOL

CONTENTS

DAVID STOREY

Like Günter Grass and David Mercer, David Storey was an art student before he became a writer. Probably a training in a field where the whole work of art can make an instantaneous impact on the viewer produces habits and inclinations which survive when the artist moves on to writing – producing artifacts which work quite differently on the reader or audience, unrolling in front of him a series of separate impacts. While the play-in-performance contains more visual elements than the novel – set, lighting, costumes, faces, bodies and movements all contributing as directly as the playwright's words to the audience's experience – the novel can accommodate very much more verbal description than the play, and there is a more direct connection between the writer's words and the pictures that form in the reader's mind. There are no other personalities, pictures or ideas to get in the way.

David Storey has said 'I feel I'm more a novelist than a playwright. The sentimental attachment is always to a novel. But I think the thing is dead on its feet. The ones that succeed rely more intensely on the visual conception of what's going on, largely because the social conception has virtually disappeared. The nineteenth century novel really was a novel of manners – the way a man dressed, for instance, could tell you a great deal about him and his position, his world, his temperament – whereas this is no longer so. Today there is no kind of cohesive social gesture which illustrates or opens up a wide aspect of society, which in a way disarms the novel itself. So you're left with either the interior element – endless subjective novels – or what we're going for in this country, imitation novels, rather like Angus Wilson. Using an old conception of a novel and trying to animate it with new but in the end basically conventional material.'

To some extent he had the feeling of going to the novel

7

because there was nothing else to go to. 'I find what the novel means to me, its significance, is very strong, but I don't know how one can express it strongly any more. All that prose somehow gets in the way. Unless it is invested with a tremendous intellectual energy from someone like Bellow. Apart from that I can't see how a novel can acquire a new kind of unity with all these disconnected bits and pieces. The social bond has gone now. Either you go back to writing – like most of my contemporaries – conventional nineteenth century novels or just write purely subjectively, an esoteric piece of prose.'

The attraction, then, of drama might lie partly in the refuge it provides from 'all that prose'. The son of a miner, he had been a bus-conductor and a footballer – amongst many other things – before he started writing novels, and he wrote about seven before he had any success.

'I think *Sporting Life* was about the eighth novel I'd written and I got so tired of trying to get them published that after *Sporting Life* had been turned down about eight times, I thought "Well I've got nothing left here, perhaps I'm really a dramatist". I was then teaching in Islington and during one half term I took time off and wrote a play. I didn't feel I'd got very far, and left it and went on with *Sporting Life*. Two years later it was published. Then there was a backlog of novels, two of which came out during the next three years, *Flight into Camden and Radcliffe*. Then I set to work on another novel which took me about four years to write and got nowhere. In 1966 a boy who had worked at the Royal Court wrote to me to say he'd seen a copy of my play at the theatre some years before – and that he had taken over the Traverse Theatre in Edinburgh, and would I mind if he did the play there. Rather as a result of the Traverse production the Court did a production of it the following summer.'

It was in 1958 that he had written the play, which he called *To Die with the Philistines*. Then in 1960, when he was twenty-seven, his first two novels *This Sporting Life* and *Flight into Camden* were both published and both won important prizes. In 1964 there were plans for a production of his play at the Royal Court, and he did more work on it, changing the title to *The Restoration of Arnold Middleton*, but it was not actually staged until November 1966, when Gordon MacDougall directed it at the Traverse, Edinburgh, with David

8

Collings as Arnold and Marian Diamond as his wife, Joan. The production at the Court followed in July 1967, directed by Robert Kidd, with Jack Shepherd as Arnold and Eileen Atkins as Joan (a part taken over by June Barry when the production transferred to the Criterion at the end of August). Harold Hobson hailed it as 'the best first play produced by the English Stage Company since *Look Back in Anger*.'

All David Storey's subsequent plays – *In Celebration* (1969) *The Contractor* (1969) *Home* (1970) and *The Changing Room* (1971) had been directed by Lindsay Anderson, whose first contact with Storey came when they worked together on the film *This Sporting Life*. 'We spent about two and a half years, I think, making that. It was the first time Lindsay had directed a feature film, it was the first time I'd written one, and the first time Karel Reisz had produced one, and the first time Richard Harris had ever taken the lead. So it was a very exploratory period for all of us, really, and I think we reached an understanding through what might be called the nightmare of making that particular film.

'I was very reluctant to script the book as it was and really wanted to use it as a starting-off point, and I think Lindsay's tendency with actors and with writers is to let them have their head, and if what happens is real, then he accepts it, and if it's not, he'll say so, rather than determine beforehand what's required – I mean that's the objective. It's an empirical way of working. So I can imagine some actors at the beginning of a production feeling perhaps at a loss as to what's going on; gradually however a shape evolves – organically – from both them and the material, determining precisely what structure is there and controlling it, saying yes or no. With a play Lindsay accepts the text and then that's it basically. With a film too I think he works very closely from a script, whereas other directors tend to use a script merely as a stepping-off ground and frequently abandon it. I think *This Sporting Life* was something of a special case because neither of us knew what the other was like or really understood the material in terms of making a film of it. It wasn't until Richard Harris appeared on the scene that there was any kind of real catalyst. His response to it was organic, a complete emotional commitment. My own attitude to the material was one of detachment. I didn't want to go through it all again. I think Richard's great value was to bring us back to the material of the book. This is what we responded to. And being able to express that clearly and directly in a way we could get hold of and work from.

'Richard had been identifying with the book because when Lindsay went out to see him in the South Seas when he was making *Mutiny on the Bounty* – he'd spent six months there filming – he'd learnt great chunks of the book off by heart. It's not a book anyone would particularly care to learn by heart.'

The plans to produce *The Restoration of Arnold Middleton* in 1964 originated out of Anderson's asking Storey whether he had ever thought of writing for the stage, but what actually triggered a very productive period of play-writing was the experience of finally seeing *The Restoration of Arnold Middleton* in performance. 'And the plays really came out after that. Having been bogged down with a novel which I'd worked at obsessively for three or four years, when *Arnold Middleton* came, it offered an alternative – just seeing it on the stage resulted in several more plays popping out, six or seven. We're gradually working through them at the moment. *The Contractor* was written immediately after *Arnold Middleton* had been on at the Court, and when I'd finished *The Contractor* I was struck by the image of the white table at the end, a white metalwork table which is left on the stage. I went back to the novel and perhaps two or three weeks later sat down one morning and thought of the table sitting by itself and thought "Well that's the beginning of something" and wrote a description of a metalwork table sitting by itself on a stage with two white chairs, bringing on a chap after a little while – somebody has to appear – who sits down, followed a moment later by someone else – he can't sit there alone too long. It really began like that, and it was written about the same time. *In Celebration* was also written either during or just before – in a few days. I wrote two plays called *Home*, and this is the better of the two, I believe. And then I went back to the novel.'

The facility for writing as quickly as this was obviously acquired through working on the novels. Some of the plays grow directly out of the novels. *The Contractor* grew out of *Radcliffe*, where the two main characters get jobs with a firm of tent contractors which, like the one in the play, employs a great many social misfits. Some of the workmen even have the same names in both novel and play. But for David Storey dramatic dialogue is something generically different from dialogue in fiction. 'I think they're essentially different. I don't think you can transpose literary dialogue into dramatic dialogue. It has to have a different dimension. In a novel it's more leisurely. It's a different conception of what dialogue has to do and what it means.'

One of the key differences between them is that in the novel the reader need not be particularly aware – unless the writer wants him to be – of characters who are present during a scene but not contributing to it by speaking or reacting. In the theatre everyone on stage needs somehow to be participating in whatever is going on. This is something Storey learned from Lindsay Anderson's reaction to some scenes he wrote for *This Sporting Life*.

'We discussed them and he said "Yes that's good, but what are these other three characters doing while these two are talking?" In my naïve literary fashion, I'd shoved them to the back of the room. In a novel you tend to forget the silent characters while you get on with the active ones. If no-one speaks for five minutes it doesn't matter, whereas you can't have people fidgeting around on a stage waiting to come out with a line whenever it's required. It was only then I appreciated that when you're actually watching dialogue, it has to have a completely different inner dynamic, that everyone has to be engaged in some way or other even if they are passive – they've got to be engaged in a way that's just as important, as informative, as the people who are talking. The moment you accept that that's essential, the material begins to create itself. The moment someone is hanging around doing nothing, you realize something's gone wrong somewhere, the play's losing its momentum, and you've got to think carefully about what's happening. Writing dialogue's so easy you can go on for pages and pages, pouring the stuff out, and it's all interesting stuff to read, but to ask actors to give it cohesion is a different matter. With a film it's perhaps even more important, because it's got to be much briefer and tighter.'

But though it may sometimes have let him down, David Storey had always had a good flair for picturing what might be happening between the actors speaking his dialogue. Thanks partly perhaps to his experience of painting, he could form in his mind a three-dimensional image of how the interrelationships might be brought to physical realization. 'When I went back to *Arnold Middleton* and read it through, there were passages where it broke down for the reason I've mentioned; a couple of characters had been shoved back while the others got on with what they had to do. When I rewrote it, I had that kind of discipline much more consciously in mind.'

But the essential quality of his work comes, above all, from the characteristic balance he achieves between the literary and the visual. Structure is particularly important in his plays: their overall shape is almost sculptured. *The Contractor* takes its form from the erection and dismantling of the tent. After starting with an empty stage, we see the tent being put up and then being prepared for the wedding breakfast. This takes place in the interval between Act II and Act III, and the lights next go up on the chaos of empty bottles, dirty glasses and plates, damaged decorations and overturned furniture that the wedding guests have left. This is cleared up, the tent is taken down and we end, as we began, with an empty stage. *In Celebration* also centres on a celebration meal, which again takes place in the interval. The play is about a family reunion occasioned by the fortieth wedding anniversary of a coalminer and his wife. As the play begins, one of their three sons is arriving in the heavily-furnished living-room of their home. The other two arrive, the conversation between sons, parents and neighbours produces a series of insights into the lives they are all leading, and we see that those of the parents and neighbours have changed very little since the sons, now all in their thirties, were children. They stay overnight but leave in the morning. The excitement over, the parents resume their lives.

In *The Contractor* a great deal of cutting was done but in *The Changing Room* the focus is wider, taking in all thirteen members of a professional rugby team, the cleaner of the changing room, the trainers, the referee and the club manager and chairman. Again, though the play is about the people, its shape – like that of Wesker's *The Kitchen* – is determined by the place, and though the place (unlike the tent in *The Contractor*) has a continuing existence both before and after the action, it comes to life only at the time of the game, and what we see is constructed around two busy climaxes, with the players changing first into their rugby clothes and,

DAVID STOREY

later, out of them. Again the main climax of action – the game itself – is excluded from the play, and again we begin and end very quietly, this time with the old cleaner, who never watches the game but whose life centres on the changing room. The wooden benches, the clothes-pegs, the towels, the rugby boots, socks, singlets and shorts, and the physical actions, including massage and the referee's inspection, contribute to the life of the play on almost exactly the same level as the words.

Because place, objects and actions are so very important in Storey's plays, especially *The Contractor* and *The Changing Room*, some people have the impression that Lindsay Anderson is involved in the preparation of the text, but he is not. All the plays produced so far were written before Anderson did his first production of a Storey play – *In Celebration* in 1969. 'I'd say the quality he brings to them is of clarity, directness – allowing them to live their own life, and not imposing an interpretation on them which either is alien, or is more or less his own, or even the author's. He allows the material to speak for itself and doesn't accentuate one interpretation at the expense of others.'

The close working relationship with Anderson has been extremely valuable to Storey. 'It's the kind of relationship you tend not to explore, because the more you look at it, the more mechanical it might become. I think broadly we both start off from opposite positions. Lindsay starts off from a kind of Tolstoyan viewpoint, a total picture of whatever you're doing, whereas I'm inclined to start off from a detail and work up towards a complete picture – all being well. In terms of actual work we arrive at a common ground from opposite corners. We never actually discuss what it's all about. The whole thing works without any kind of exposition beforehand. It's really an intuitive response.

'In terms of cutting, this is very useful. I write the plays and then leave them for three or four months and then take them out and read them through again, and if it strikes a bell anywhere, I type them out and cut them down but leave pieces in whenever I'm unsure. I find Lindsay's good at placing the overall structure and indicating the bits which really do impede it. Particularly with *In Celebration*, where there was

13

a formidable amount of material: cutting gave it a much clearer definition.'

In *The Contractor* a great deal of cutting was done but in fact most of the cuts were restored in rehearsal. 'The play was all conceived in terms of work. On the page it seems that nothing's going on – an author's self-indulgence – but in rehearsal we gradually put it all back, with a little bit more besides.

'Each play, I suppose, is different to that extent. *In Celebration* is a more literary play. It's basically people sitting in a room talking about themselves and other people. Although the effect, if it works, is a theatrical one, you'd say its antecedents were more literary than theatrical, and therefore as a text it's much more amenable to cutting; whereas *The Contractor's* such a physical thing that you can't really relate the text to it directly. The conception is more theatrical. I suppose one learns from all this. In *The Changing Room*, for example, which technically is a very difficult play to do, with a great deal of physical action which has to be carefully co-ordinated, we didn't have to remove a line. Apart from an odd word, to let an actor leave, or to facilitate his entry, there were no additions either.'

Do they happen in very different ways to you – the different kinds of conception?

'They tend to pop out at the same time, so it's really a question of moving from one to the other. They're all, in a way, traditional plays because they all have one set, one environment, and everything happens within it. In the past I've tried to write plays where there was a constant change of environment – Shakespeare's change every minute, don't they? – rather like a novel, where you move from one event to another, but I found – until recently – the unity of one place was all I could manage. Given a set at the beginning, I found it terribly hard to get out of it. A play I've completed recently – *Cromwell* – achieves a certain success, I think, in this direction.'

To say that the plays have become less literary and more visual as Storey has developed would be an over-simplification, but whereas *Home*, for instance, grew out of an image, *The Restoration of Arnold Middleton* started out of an anecdote – 'Which again, is literary. I tend to start novels from anecdotes, and plays from a first line, which is followed by a second. I think *Arnold*, in that sense, is pretty close to a novel. It exists in its own terms perhaps as a play, but when I watch it, I get the feeling it's written by someone who should really write novels.

'Similarly with *In Celebration*. I think this reveals itself particularly in one of the characters, played in the original production by Brian Cox, who has to sit in silence for virtually the whole play, not because the author doesn't think he's important, but because he hasn't got anything to say, or if he has, he can't express it. Someone who'd been an actor or brought up in a theatrical tradition would never have written a character like that, knowing how difficult, technically, it is for an actor to play that part. He has to fill it with a kind of energy which is totally static, and yet he must never be boring. John Gielgud had a similar task before him in *Home* with Harry, with all his Oh yeses and his silences and his incapacity to say anything very clearly. Although once it is achieved it is very moving and perhaps even eloquent in its own way, its roots are essentially literary. Now I know more about the theatre, I would never dare to write parts like that again, making that kind of demand on an actor. . . . They're all plays of understatement in a way and if you don't get what they're understating, then you've really had it, because there's nothing great going on on the surface. It's all got to be going on in the audience's mind, particularly with *Home*.'

The effectiveness of *In Celebration* also depends largely on how far it succeeds in getting the action going in the audience's mind. It seems as though the play is leading towards a big showdown between mother and eldest son, but this never comes. 'I thought the point of the play was that there was no kind of conventional confrontation. In a way the explosion has already taken place off or outside or away, and this is the aftermath. If you compare it – however tentatively – with Ibsen in terms of approaching psychological realities, Ibsen is writing about a time in history before the explosion has occurred, the bomb is festering away inside and eventually goes off. With *In Celebration*, it's not a question of stripping off hypocrisies, deceits and complacencies, but of asking what do you do with the people afterwards – and *are* they really deceit and hypocrisy and complacency? Aren't the parents, for instance, in *In Celebration* more "real", less pretentious and more effective as people than their three so-called emancipated sons? The truth of the play perhaps lies in *that* confrontation, rather than the one that is seemingly avoided on the surface.

'I would have said that the play could only have been written fifty or a hundred years after Ibsen in that sense. There really is no stripping away any more. The illusions in that sense have gone. People stick to the lying. The bomb is there and we no longer need the explosion, the ripping out of the heart and head. It really is a question of soldiering on, or of compromising, or forgiving, as the play suggests at the end. I don't know whether this is too literary or not, an author's self-indulgence. If it is, then the play is a failure.

'I think *The Contractor*'s a similar case of a deliberate withdrawal from drama in that sense. Again, all the confrontations that could take place there, are, if you like, skilfully avoided, because the actual conception of the play is directed towards that end rather than explosion and revelation.'

Home in some sense arrives at a point towards which the earlier plays had been striving. *The fact of non-confrontation is made integral to the conception and to the nature of the characters. They have to be people who don't, who can't confront what there is to confront, and that's the subject, isn't it?*

'That may be true. I think *Home*'s limitations are there for everyone to see. Whereas with the other plays I feel there is a lurking ambition to broaden the conception and to set the limits a bit higher than they have been set. Perhaps because it was written so quickly, within a couple of days, *Home* doesn't try to shift its premisses and is probably more of an entity.'

When he started writing it he had not decided where the metalwork table was, or what the characters were going to be like. 'It was only when the ladies came on that I began to suspect they were in a mental home and not where I thought they were, in a hotel. When the ladies appear there's this terrible reversal of roles – the women behave like men and the men more like women. It was when they began to refer explicitly to their various ailments that I realized they were slightly unstable. I think that's where the reviews did a disservice to the play in saying that it was about a madhouse. It's a given premiss, if you like, but in fact it's not the material of the play itself, and to say it's a mental home is a way of distancing the audience from the play. It isn't just that it diminishes the play and the conception, making it a special case, but it sets you away from the emotion, from the suffering; whereas the characters, I would think, are those you might meet in the street any day.

'I wouldn't think any of the characters are actually insane. They could quite as easily have been outside as inside, I feel. In fact, when we did the play at Brighton and stayed at these terrible hotels, there were thousands of them all round us. You know, the same dialogue. And when Sir John and Sir Ralph stopped rehearsing, you were never quite sure whether they were talking or rehearsing. There is a sort of disclaimer really when it becomes firmly a play about a mental home. It makes the audience feel apart from it – "These people are mad and we're not mad. How extraordinary the things that mad people do!" I think people in mental homes in real life are slightly different from this, just from their aspect. You'd never find anyone as convivial as that in a mental home. In fact most of them – when they aren't actively deranged – are passive and silent.'

Storey's speed in writing plays is all the more remarkable when compared with the time he has invested in the novels. He has toiled at these almost like a miner, laboriously digging them out, bit by bit, from deep underground. A novel called *A Temporary Life* which has not yet been published, took two years to write, and *Pasmore*, which appeared in 1972, was a by-product of a much larger novel he had been working at for seven years. 'I have a strong resistance to reading anything I've written until I absolutely have to. I was prepared to spend four or five years on this particular novel. It was one that I wanted to do when I was very young, and this was a conception I'd built up to slowly through *Sporting Life* and *Camden* and *Radcliffe*, with varying degrees of success. Then I sat down and wrote it but found when I came to read it, it didn't work. It must be seven years since I began and I'm still writing it. *Pasmore* is a kind of interim statement. I've written several novels on or around this theme. Three of them are virtually – not the same novel, but they involve the same situation and characters in three different conceptions. The great bulk of work from which they are detached is the main thing, and in a way the plays stem from that – little shoots off the side.'

The original theme of this novel was the split in Storey's life which became evident when he was a student, spending the week trying to paint (following his training at the Slade School) and playing professional rugby at the week-ends, in Yorkshire. 'I couldn't see any connection between the reality of the one thing, a very rough and hard game played for money, and the terrible reality of the other, a completely introverted event calling on – as I then thought – great powers of self-absorption. The novel I wanted to write was about a character in whom this feeling of sub-division had been resolved, where these two elements were in some sort of equilibrium. The division between those who can make society work for them and those who can't was so marked in my life at that time that I felt driven into writing about it.

'This division was not just one of temperament but could be reflected in society as well. In the coal-mining area I came from, an artist was a fairly suspect fellow doing something for no apparent purpose and with no tangible reward – here were these men working down the pit all week and providing funds for people like me to go and paint pictures, which *they* could do at week-ends, if they wanted, as well as work. I felt this division both within my own family and the world around – and the corresponding pressure was to find some kind of resolution. *This Sporting Life* was a first attempt at writing about a man who could make society work but not much else. *Flight into Camden* was an attempt to write about someone who had an intuitive response to life and not much else, who couldn't really get on with people. *Radcliffe* was where these two characters were brought together. *Radcliffe* was the intuitive outcast, with something of an artistic temperament, and the other character was a man with a good appetite for life, a sort of blindness to life and who got on with it, but felt that something else was missing. This large novel was an attempt to bring the two elements together within the life of one individual. I suppose that theme is in the plays, certainly in Arnold Middleton, the chap who quietly goes mad while he maintains a kind of charade till he can't relate to anything. In *In Celebration* there's an attempt, I believe, to break it up. That was the most deliberately written of the plays. Beforehand I decided there would be three arguments in the play. One was the ascetic, silent temperament; there would also be the latently revolutionary one; the third man who, rather like Harold Wilson, says this is the best of all possible worlds and you've got to make a go of it.

'I suppose, looking back over all this work, I tend to see it – not wholly for defensive reasons – as a kind of failure. I was very much aware in the past, for instance, of trying to match one kind of life with another – an inner life with an outer; or a working-class life and its instincts with a middle-class life and its urges towards reason and the status quo – and I couldn't in the end, or I can't now, see any resolution. I've had enough time and opportunity to see that there are great themes that can be expressed in literature and drama, yet – perhaps through a romantic addiction to the role of the artist, perhaps through a simple lack of talent – I've never quite made it. I still see it all in working-class terms, as competition, like a runner trying to get some impossible record; or a boxer fighting for a championship: I write every day – in one sense – in order to keep 'fit'. I'm not sure it's the best thing to do, or even required. A coalminer puts in his shift each day; an athlete trains to maintain a certain consistency and standard, as a stepping-off board to something higher. To ask me to take a day off from writing is like asking a prospector to give up – if only temporarily – the rights to his claim, when it might *just* be that day that fate has destined him to dig up a kingsize nugget. On the whole he knows, doesn't he, the chances are against it?'

Storey may regard himself – perhaps not unduly – as a pessimist; but it's interesting that there is one writer who, for him, typifies a successful synthesis between the two kinds of life. Günter Grass and he have more than an art school background in common: they have both been trying energetically – as very few recent English writers have tried—to work both as novelists and in the theatre. Storey feels a very warm admiration for Grass.

'When I met him I really thought "That's how you live", because he seemed an absolute peasant in his response to life – it was so direct, two feet on the earth and solid. And yet underneath it was a tremendous shrewdness. He has a real gift for writing and you felt when he cooked, or when he wrote poems or when he drew, the same kind of animal conviction came into it. Even watching him smoke a cigarette had the same effect. You felt everything he did had this reality about it. People like that are the world's magicians. They have a kind of elemental magic about them – Picasso is another – they come from the centre of the earth somewhere and they just have it.'

JEAN ANOUILH

No playwright has bridged more successfully between the highbrow and middlebrow audience than Jean Anouilh. His plays may no longer have the same appeal to the intellectuals that they had in the late thirties and the forties but he is still popular. In 1971 he had three plays on in Paris simultaneously – two new plays, *Les Poissons rouges* and *Ne reveillez pas Madame*, and a revival at the Comédie Française of his *Becket*. Most of the twenty-seven plays he has written have been seen in all the major theatrical capitals of the world, and if we had statistics of how many performances various plays received in various countries, they would probably show that his have been more popular than the work of any other living playwright with any claim to seriousness.

Not that his popularity has been immune to changes of fashion. None of his plays were staged in Paris between 1962 *(Le Foire d'empoigne)* and 1969 *(Cher Antoine)* and he stopped writing for three years. 'Theatre captures me by its smell, and as those six years went by without any productions of my plays, I needed to rediscover theatre, to find the smell again. One day I was passing through Marseilles, and they were presenting a play in an old theatre, and I sniffed that strange smell, that bad old smell. I entered once again into the atmosphere of the theatre. It becomes a world where one doesn't think about what's going on outside – it's extraordinary, it simply doesn't count. Perhaps you notice that the weather's nice, that it's August. Any rehearsal is very much like any other but you enter into it completely, and the world outside no longer exists. I still remember that day. I told myself I must direct a play and I went back to Paris and I directed not one of my own plays but a play by Roger Vitrac, a friend of mine who died in 1952 without achieving any success.'

Anouilh went on directing plays by other writers in Paris and enjoying the freedom from the anxieties of having his own work presented to the critics. 'It's like sitting for an examination every single year. When you've done that all your life there comes a time when you just don't want to know whether you did well, whether you got eighteen marks out of twenty, or nought. I don't care any more.'

After a seven year gap in performances and a three year gap in writing he was naturally nervous about *Cher Antoine*, but it was an immediate success, and it is so closely in line with his earlier work that no one would have known about the discontinuity. As in so many of his plays, the focus is on life inside the theatre. But he always writes with his tongue in his cheek, and it is always dangerous to equate any of his characters with himself. 'People say they are stories in which my presence can be felt, especially the last two, but that's both true and untrue. You always put in something of yourself, but you borrow from other people, and you end up with something that isn't yourself, though everyone thinks it is. In Paris you have to have fun, and in *Cher Antoine* I amused myself a bit at the expense of the people who always say "That's him" by writing about a playwright. There are jokes for the initiated, like the line about this writer putting Germans into the play because he'd been in Germany. But most people didn't know that I had adapted Kleist's *Das Käthchen von Heilbronn*. But in spite of these jokes for the initiated, I write for the public.'

In his view, *Cher Antoine*, *Les Poissons rouges* and *Ne reveillez pas Madame*, which were all 'written in a sort of delight at having rediscovered the theatre', represent a slightly different kind of drama from that of his earlier plays, but he would like to go on to write plays in which the difference is more marked. 'I still have one more to write which is in line with the last three. Afterwards I want to do something else. Perhaps that's presumptuous, but you had George Bernard Shaw, who went on writing until he was ninety – right up to the end in fact. I've always thought there was an age when one had to stop. One has no more imagination, no more strength.

'What I need in order to write another kind of drama – if I'm not too old – is to be exiled, put in prison, something that would stop me from picturing the production. I don't write for an actor, I transcribe a performance that I visualize: I write a scene as I imagine it being played out in front of me. If for some reason destiny decreed that my plays were never again to be produced and that I was to write a different sort of play that I was never going to direct, I'd be able to write quite differently, benefiting from the freedom of not having to visualize it on the stage. I've been doing it so long that I can't help imagining the performance. And that's how I write it. It's like making a shorthand transcription of a play no-one else knows, with me as the only member of the audience. Paul Claudel, the old French playwright who wrote those mysterious and beautiful plays, was French Ambassador in Tokyo, and he was writing at a time when it was unthinkable that his plays would ever be presented in the fashionable boulevard theatre – which was dominated by writers like Henri Bernstein. So in that freedom he wrote plays that were absolutely mad, because he could imagine whatever he liked. Except for *L'Otage*, *L'Annonce faite a Marie* and *L'Echange*, they weren't staged until the forties. So he had his pockets full of plays. I've always said "I must save up for the future". I'd like to have five plays up my sleeve to be performed when I'm old. But when Claudel was seventy he had a new play produced in Paris every year. When I was a young man, a year never went by without a new production of a play by Claudel that had been in print since 1910. But my reserve stock consists of a single play. I must write some more. But that's what theatre is – to write for immediate production. After all, both Shakespeare and Molière did; they knew a play had to be finished within a fortnight – otherwise the theatre would have been empty. And that's a very good discipline for a playwright.'

People who remember the impact of Anouilh's early plays in the forties are likely to feel ambivalent about them, because the very qualities that made for the theatrical magic they generated depend on a distortion of reality which it is difficult to forgive. The purity and innocence of the young lovers was always contrasted simplistically with the gross, lip-smacking sensuality of their corrupt parents. Death was presented as the one attractive alternative to a life which seemed intolerable, not because the young heroes and heroines would be coarsened by the process of growing older but because they had no other refuge from the generation that was maliciously set on

destroying their innocence in the process of finding fodder
for its own coarse appetites. Plays like *Eurydice* (1941, known
over here as *Point of Departure*) and *Antigone* (1943) now
seem very strange to Anouilh himself. 'I get the impression I'm
reading plays by my son – a young man who isn't me. There
are certain things one still feels, because one's the same person,
but those early plays seem awfully remote. I wrote plays which
don't seem so far away, but everything I wrote in that early
period, was very spiteful and derisive. I needed to sneer, to
write sour comedy. Now I feel less like that. It was a sort of
rejection of life by a young man who'd been a bit hurt by it.
Death is the only thing that corrects the balance of things that
have gone bad or erases the memory of them, but after a while
you notice that death is just as absurd and just as dirty as life.
It's equally ridiculous – not at all beautiful.

'But you must never confuse my own life with what I write,
even though there is a secret zone or another creative life
which is equally important, equally true, and this is perhaps
one's real life. My plays are my only refuge. It's strange. I
can't remember dates, I have no memory for things that happen to me. I'm the complete amnesiac. Everything that happens
becomes remote. I remember nothing of my life before I was
twelve. I'm completely asocial, and I forget social engage-
ments, refuse to see people. But sometimes I meet someone –
because I know everyone and everyone knows me – and when
we say "Good morning. How are you?" I say to myself
"This person is someone I detest, someone who's done something horrible to me" and I can't remember what! My plays
are my only landmarks. For instance I remember the circum-
stances in which a play was written. I remember what happened at the time of writing *Antigone* or *Eurydice*. That's my
calendar. It would be possible to write two parallel biographies
of an author, one of the ordinary life he leads, the other of his
secret life, of his creative sensitivity which also has a childhood, an adolescence and a maturity which bear no resem-
blance to his own childhood, adolescence and maturity.'

Disgust at life in his plays does not correspond to his own
feelings about life. In his book *20th Century French Drama*
(Columbia University Press) the American critic, David Gross-
vogel, suggests that Anouilh is like Montherlant in adumbrat-
ing a pattern in which the hero is called on

to resume his virginity – that is, to give up establishing the illusion in this world either through the suicide of a return to his former being, or through the consecration of death in which the dream will endure. That is why so many end in a debauch of self-disfiguration during which words flow like blood from a gashed artery until the victim is dead. Only in death (that of non-believers) can the sham, the shame, and the world that made it, cease. Only in death will the illusion be reality. Here is truly Montherlant's "thirst for nothingness".

Anouilh's reaction to this was 'I don't think I've ever had this thirst for nothingness. Let's try to see things clearly: every young man of sixteen or seventeen thinks it would be better and simpler to die. But as soon as I came to grips with the weight of things, especially the weight of people, everything was different. I was a student for a year and a half and then I was a father – I've been a father all my life. I had beautiful children. And yet I wouldn't say this nihilism is insincere, or just a literary device. But equally I don't think it was a thirst for nothingness. There were times when I was tired of life, like everyone else, and thought it would be better to sleep. But that doesn't correspond to a thirst for nothingness in my own life. It's more like part of the creative life in which I had these feelings without knowing them in my terrestrial life. In any case I doubt whether I could have afforded those deep feelings. On the contrary, I had to build my life very seriously, defending it from other people. And there's something in that that doesn't go with the Nirvana thoughts of a man lying on a divan smoking cigarettes and thinking it would be better for him to die. I believe in a moral health which isn't in accord with that. But certainly, since it's in so many of my plays, it must have existed in my other life, the creative life. It was my first response to experience. These were the plays of a very young man and I remained a very young man for a very long time. I only began to understand things during the war or after the war, when I was thirty. As a young man I understood nothing. I couldn't have told you what a political party was. I knew nothing. I was just waiting for the Liberation. What was happening in France was terrible. We had to live through two years that corresponded to the Revolution of 1789 or 1792 and 93. At the age of thirty-four I didn't even know what the difference was between a Communist and a Socialist!'

Sometimes the connection between the two kinds of life can be closer than the artist himself realizes and it is possible that Anouilh's plays provided an outlet for emotions and attitudes which would otherwise have bulked larger in his relationships both with other people and with himself. It is odd though that poverty is such a recurring theme in his early plays – money being associated with corruption – when he had so little experience of what it felt like to be poor. He was the son of a tailor in Bordeaux. He went to Paris to study law and for a time he worked as Louis Jouvet's secretary. 'I was one of the first publicity agents in France; at the age of nineteen I was earning 3,000 francs a month, which is equivalent to 3,000 new francs today. I was twenty-two when my first play was produced. It was very successful but I didn't appreciate what was happening. Later on when I went through some bad years, I realized what luck I'd had to be so successful so young.

'After my first play I decided to give up public relations, and then I knew poverty, but it was only the poverty of making do with a coffee and a sandwich instead of a proper meal. It didn't harm me at all. It's through other people that one arrives at the knowledge necessary to write a character like Thérèse in La Sauvage, a play of mine which was massacred in London. But personally I've always felt rich, even when I had nothing. I never had a complex about poverty, although the money didn't start coming in till I was forty, forty-four. But I know what poverty is because I lived among poor people for a long time, and experienced it deeply through them, but the movement of revolt against it in the plays was never a personal one. In Poor Bitos, which was done in London with Donald Pleasence, people thought there was something of me in Bitos. That's not true at all. His political viewpoint is the opposite of mine. Even from the human point of view there's no correspondence. I detest men like that.'

In 1932 it was much more unusual than it is today for a playwright of twenty-two to have his work produced, but by then Anouilh had already been obsessed with the theatre for fourteen years. 'My theatrical life began when I was eight. It was the year of the Spanish 'flu epidemic and I caught it.

JEAN ANOUILH

One evening on the esplanade at Royan, near the pier, there was a puppeteer with very large hand-puppets who was doing an artless production of *Romeo and Juliet*. I was taken ill during the performance. I had a temperature, I was shivering, I thought I was going to die. I was delirious for eight days, during which this production of *Romeo and Juliet* went on in my head, mixed up with feverish fantasies. And even now when I think of that play, I still picture those puppets and feel the emotions of that time.

'These childhood memories have enormous power. I'm sure that experience crystallized the mystery of the theatre for me, and it was the basis of my production of *Richard III*. We bought all the costumes from an old production of an opera called *The Huguenots* and we dressed everyone up in these old opera clothes. We infuriated Paris. Everyone said it was disgusting, revolting.'

Anouilh has exercised a powerful influence on the Paris theatre. His voice was one of the first to be raised in support of the original production of Beckett's *Waiting for Godot* (in Paris, January 1953) and in 1956 he turned Ionesco's *The Chairs* from a failure into a success. 'It was playing next door to my *Ornifle*, and the manager of the theatre said that no-one was coming to see it. So I wrote an article on *The Chairs* on the bottom right-hand side of the front page of *Le Figaro* and the next day the theatre was full. Things changed overnight. Now whenever a play does bad business I get asked to write on it. I have done it four or five times and it has always worked.

'I was very affected by that style of theatre, very interested, but it brought plenty of bad plays – pseudo-Becketts and pseudo-Ionescos. It provided a dangerous aesthetic for young people who don't have the genius of Beckett and Ionesco.' It was probably the imitation of Beckett and Ionesco that provoked Anouilh into writing a parody of that kind of play in *L'Hurluberlu (The Fighting Cock)*. 'One has the right to admire and then make a parody, to do something like that even if it is only to amuse oneself. It's not malicious.'

His first plays were directed by Pierre Fresnay. Then in 1937 *Le Voyageur sans bagages* was directed by Georges Pitoëff, whom Anouilh describes as 'the only theatrical genius I've ever known'. After directing *La Sauvage* in 1938, Pitoëff

died in 1939, and a long partnership began between Anouilh
and André Barsacq, who revived *Bal des voleurs* in 1940, going
on to direct *Le Rendez-vous de Senlis, Antigone, Roméo et
Jeannette, L'Invitation au Château, Colombe* and *Médée*. 'I left
Barsacq because whispering into someone's ear every five
minutes saying "It would be better to do it this way" is not
the same thing as to take charge and say "No, this is how it's
done", and explain directly to the actors. It's not possible for
me to direct my own plays abroad because I speak no foreign
languages. And then you get strange things happening because
the director can transform the whole feeling of the play. I've
had some splendid surprises. There was a play called *The
Waltz of the Toreadors* which was a complete flop in France.
I came to London to work with Peter Hall. I sat in the stalls
and got the impression that I understood English because I
recognized everything in the text. All the laughs came exactly
where I wanted them, and where I hadn't got them in Paris.'

Sometimes plays have done better when the production
departs from his original intentions. 'Les Poissons rouges is a
play which I failed to direct as drily and cynically as I
intended, but one day we had the idea of staging it with two
comedians, two clowns. Since then it's had three hundred and
fifty performances and it's always sold out. So it works. It's
very funny. In Germany they produced it according to my
intentions, with villains, heroes and traitors. It didn't work.
It needs to be done with two comedians. The director changed
it into something serious – you see, a director can make or
break a play.'

Anouilh's methods of working have changed over the forty
years he's been writing for the theatre. 'In my early plays, I
tried to construct with great precision, knowing exactly where
I was going. But when you have everything worked out –
when you're hired to write the dialogue for a film which
already has a scenario – you need the qualities of a writer who
can construct secretly, apparently letting everything happen
by chance but actually foreseeing everything. It bores me if
I know where the plot is going exactly. But I think that when
I write a play, I don't have an exact subject that I could tell
anyone, but I have a character or two and, above all, an
atmosphere.

'I write quickly when something works. Either it fails completely or it goes very fast. I have the impression that it's a play which already exists and which I saw a long time ago; I try to remember it as if I had to tell the story to someone. I feel as if I'd forgotten the details but that I'll rediscover them in writing. I always feel I'm rediscovering something that already exists.'

The development of a plot can be shaped by something which happens quite by chance. He started working on *La Répétition (The Rehearsal)*, which has a particularly involved construction, when he was in the Midi, near Toulon. 'My plays always start with a monologue because I don't know what I'm going to do. I saw that woman, I had an idea of the little governess, and of her husband, of a couple. The idea came to me that they were wearing fancy dress, then I thought they could be in costume because they were rehearsing a play. Then I began to write. Then it had to be a play by Marivaux. I remember, I took my car and went to Toulon to the bookshop and asked for plays by Marivaux and they gave me Volume Two because they didn't have Volume One. I went back to sit in the car and opened the book at *The Double Inconstancy*. I remembered the play a little. I turned over three pages, found a scene, and that's how I went on with the play. It was quite by chance that I hit on *The Double Inconstancy*. If they'd given me Volume Three, I'd have written a totally different play. I didn't know how it would develop but I had that atmosphere of fashionable, hard-bitten people with one of them suddenly experiencing a different kind of love, purer. I had the feel of the play but not the details.

'Once I've written a draft, I hardly change it at all. I write very little, only for two hours in the morning, and then I stop even if it's going well – in fact especially if it's going well, because that's when you write those beautiful scenes like the ones in old plays, which go on and on. The next day I bring someone else into the scene and it changes. Then I type it in the afternoon, but I don't rewrite much. I'm lazy. Perhaps if I did more revising it would be better.'

In fact, of course, as he knows very well, it would not. He has perfected the technique of transcribing an imaginary performance to such an extent that he almost writes the audience's reaction into the script, knowing exactly when the laughs are going to come, and when the Parisian spectators are going to applaud at the end of a long speech. Watching *Ne reveillez pas Madame* at the Comédie des Champs-Elysées, I had the feeling that it was the mood and the mixture of ingredients that the audience was responding to so enthusiastically, more than the story or the characters. The young girl was still just as innocent as the young girls in his early plays and the world of the theatre just as corrupt, but on this level the play is like a fairy story. The question hardly arises of whether the characters have counterparts in the world outside. Most of all Anouilh is fortunate in the way that he seems to be able to please himself and his public at the same time, with the same well-tried but still mellow blend of comedy and pathos, past and present, theatrical theatricality and theatrical reality, nostalgia and disillusionment, sentiment and satire. And if there are many who find the old magic no longer works, there are many who find it still does.

PETER BROOK

The art of the director is a comparatively young one. Until the middle of the nineteenth century, what happened on the stage was controlled mainly by the playwright or the leading actor, and much that is carefully regulated today was left to chance. The candle-lighting that was used until the eighteen-forties left a large part of the stage in semi-darkness and when gas lighting was introduced it was the prompter who directed it. Throughout the first half of the century rehearsals had nothing like the importance they have today. Rehearsal periods were brief and they were used merely to sketch out groupings and movements of the supporting company in relation to the leading actors – not to develop characterizations or mould a *mise-en-scène*.

In the eighteen-fifties, thanks to actor-managers like Charles Kean and the Bancrofts, and to writers like Dion Boucicault and W. S. Gilbert, progress was made towards organizing acting performances, theatrical effects and lighting into a more coherent shape, but the turning point for the London theatre did not come until 1881, when the Duke of Saxe-Meiningen brought his company to Drury Lane, seven years after it had made an equally crucial impact on the Berlin theatre, showing what could be achieved in production when a director combined the talents of artist, planner and disciplin-arian. In 1890 Stanislavski watched the Duke's stage manager, Ludwig Chronegk, directing the company in a Moscow rehearsal. 'I started to imitate Chronegk,' he wrote, 'and with time I became a producer-autocrat myself, and many Russian directors began imitating me as I had imitated Chronegk.'

This then was the start of the autocratic tradition which was to survive, in England, into the middle of the present century, and, on the continent, is not dead even now. What it meant in practice was that the directors planned not only the

31

shape but the detail of his production before he had his first rehearsal with the actors. Stanislavski has described how he prepared *The Seagull*: 'I shut myself up in my study and wrote a detailed *mise-en-scène* as I felt it and as I saw and heard it with my inner eye and ear. At those moments I did not care for the feelings of the actor! I sincerely believed it was possible to tell people to live and feel as I liked them to; I wrote down directions for everybody and those directions had to be carried out. I put down everything in those production notes; how and where, in what way a part had to be interpreted and the playwright's stage directions carried out, what kind of inflections the actor had to use, how he had to move about and act, and when and how he had to cross the stage. I added all sorts of sketches for every *mise-en-scène* – exits, entries, crossings from one place to another, and so on and so forth. I described the scenery, costumes, make-up, deportment, gaits, and habits of the characters, etc.'

Later he became less dictatorial, and in any case few directors went into such meticulous preparatory detail, but generally their method was to block all the moves in advance, devoting the early rehearsals to telling the actors where to come in, when to sit down, when to get up and look out of the window. Later more detail would be imposed on them within the outline that had then been determined.

Some directors, of course, were less autocratic than others. Athene Seyler remembers working for Sir Gerald du Maurier, who at one rehearsal said to her: 'Now darling, this is your scene. Where do you want to sit and where do you want the others?' This was not so much sharing the initiative with her as handing it over to her.

It is only against this background that the importance of Peter Brook's achievement can be understood. As he says himself, 'Today you find it very hard to find a young director who works anything out on paper. He realizes that things evolve with a group. At first I was very much on my own in this directing method. I was working against the tradition, which was the tradition of the prompt book, of the director arriving with a bulky book in which it's all worked out and written down. And this was considered a sign of serious work. I resisted it, believing that this was theoretical work, that any work done by somebody before rehearsals is work done in theory. It isn't living work. The living work is done on the spot, on the floor, with the actors. I, for this reason, like to develop everything through trial and error and experiment and improvisation with the actors.'

It was in his seventh professional production, and his first at Stratford-on-Avon, *Love's Labour's Lost* in 1946, that he discarded the old method of directing. He had prepared his production very carefully, working with a model of the set and cardboard figures to represent each character. He had written down all the moves he wanted. But on the first morning of rehearsals he found that instead of helping his relationships with the actors and their relationships with each other, his annotations were merely getting in the way. He found the courage to put his script aside, and since then he has never gone back to the old method of directing.

This does not mean that he now goes to the first rehearsal of a new production with no notion in his head of what he wants. But it is difficult for him to know how the ideas, the images and the inclinations that he starts with will be articulated in the work that is done with the actors in rehearsal. He explains it by analogy, pointing to the difference between a painter's or sculptor's methods of working and a composer's. 'Before he picks up his pen a composer has a complete and detailed image in his mind of a full symphony orchestra with each line in movement. He writes down the structure which has developed almost complete in his mind, and then many musicians don't change anything. And you contrast this with a sculptor who has in front of him a big block, whose intention is that he is going to search for a certain shape within that block. But stroke for stroke he is amending and changing that intention – otherwise it would never really emerge. The greatest example of this is in the Picasso film, showing Picasso reaching the end of his intention by endless apparent empiricism – one dot leading to a line, leading to a new thing erased . . . It's as though one starts from something that one feels very strongly. One can even talk about it and define it to a degree, but it hasn't quite got a form, and you go towards that with the people concerned – amending, changing, adapting, finding – and at the end, as the form emerges, you realize that this is where you've been going from the start.'

Naturally, for actors who had grown up under the old

directorial tradition, being effectively formed by it, it was not easy to take advantage of the new freedom. 'It's only comparatively recently that a *whole* theatre, a whole new generation of actors to a man, accept a method which an older generation – almost to a man – refused. I'd say that most of the older actors I have directed, I found very difficult to work with: whether it was that they were unsympathetic, or perhaps alien, I found it hard to find any particular taste or enjoyment for their way of work. I worked as a necessary evil with lots of actors who I knew were accepting a method from me because it gave good results, but which they couldn't understand and didn't like. And I was accepting from them a sort of resistance, although I felt their approach to the work was wrongly stolid.

'Today with any young actor that I know, any actor of what I would call the new generation of English actors, this doesn't arise, because this way of work corresponds to the way they would work instinctively, even if nobody were there telling them. And in that way people like Edith Evans – and a hundred others – belong to a school in which the dream is the director who walks in on the first day in a purely dictatorial and arbitrary way and says a hundred things they can write down in the margin, which they will then take as gospel. They won't have their opinion asked, won't contribute. They will just take, and, having done that, they then expect to be left alone, pretty well. They will obediently absorb those things and then as long as they aren't changed, they've got that bit out of the way, and they concentrate on developing their work by repetition. This to me is a ghastly method, but for a school of actor, for a type of play, the sort of play that was current thirty years ago, it led to good results.'

The one actor of the old school with whom Brook found an immediate and instinctive rapport was John Gielgud. 'With us there had been a *very* deep one from the second we began to talk to one another. I remember that one of the reasons we liked working together was that both of us work very empirically. Neither of us believes in starting from a set, established plan.'

Temperamentally Gielgud is strongly disposed to a trial-and-error approach. 'It's the way he always worked – he can't think ahead, he can only work by trying, and as he has this endless series of ideas, he immediately sees every possibility, and so invariably very comic things happen at rehearsal. He starts a sentence and says "I wonder if it wouldn't be a good idea if I came in from the left . . ." And before he has finished that, his mind has got tired of the idea and so, as he's explaining it to us, it's "Or maybe I should come in from the right?" And when on the first rehearsal I said to him "John, you come in from the back," before I'd finished that, he cut me up and said "Yes, but wouldn't it be better if I'm already discovered in a chair?" And before he'd finished that I saw the advantage of him being in a chair, but that gave me the idea that maybe even better than sitting in a chair, would be him lying on his back, and I say "You mean lying on your back?" And he said "Yes, marvellous, but then if I were lying on my back, I could be wheeled in on a stretcher". We found that we were both thinking in exactly the same way – often to the dismay of the cast who would find this endless change very disturbing. By the time one had said to some of the other actors "Now, you go there and you go there, we're going to try it out this way", either John or I had seen the disadvantages, and said "It's not worth trying that. It's no good anyway. Let's try something else".

'But on the whole, what it meant was that work would be experimental, high speed, and in the course of it John would improvise. In this sense he belongs completely to the most free and modern school. He wouldn't admit this all that readily, but he does everything by pure improvisation. So he improvises in one of many different keys of playing, explores something – says "Well, the character no doubt at this moment is ferocious", and as he begins to speak the line ferociously that gives him the idea that the character really may be meaning to say that line very gently, and he does it, tastes it, by doing it in a gentle way. In this way, over the course of two or three days, an enormous number of variations have already been explored; I then found the difference between John and myself was that John would tend to carry on endlessly with this process. In fact you know that famous story of him changing moves after the last performance of a play. Because his restlessness is permanent.

'Mine is different. With me it's like a golf ball – when you play as badly as I do, once a year, at the seaside on the putting green, where the ball always goes across the hole and never in, you go round and round and round the hole until eventually you get a right hit, and the ball goes in. That is where we differ – that I do use this method to winnow away the inessential and then suddenly recognize what we're looking for. With John it's at that point, towards the end of rehearsals that I've suddenly been able to dictate to him his own performance. In other words dictate to him his own discovery, not mine. People often ask directors: "Do you tell the actor what to do, do you tell an eminent actor what to do, or does he tell you?" And of course it never works that way, but with John it's the reverse of that. In the fourth week of rehearsal I'd say to John "John, you do this line in this way", and he's delighted to be reminded because it falls into place, and he suddenly remembers that *was* the best way and that *does* tie up with what I'm doing. And that's where there has been a perfect collaboration between us, because I've been able to help him to play the performance that he really set out to play, but which he could easily have blurred for himself with over-rich material.'

This goes a long way towards explaining why five of Gielgud's best performances have been the ones in which he was directed by Brook – Angelo in *Measure for Measure* (1950), Leontes in *The Winter's Tale* (1951), Jaffier in Otway's *Venice Preserv'd* (1953), Prospero in *The Tempest* (1957), and Oedipus in Seneca's *Oedipus*, adapted by Ted Hughes (1960). 'If you look at John in films, and if you look at John in his reading, *The Seven Ages of Man* which is one of the most remarkable things he's done, you see very clearly the difference between the very simple, very true and very realistic actor that there is contained in John, and John's extravagances or mannerisms, as they've been called at different times. The part of John that's a director is always concerned with the show as a whole, so when he directs himself he always neglects his own performance – he knows this – and consequently whenever he directs himself he always goes out on an enormous tour, recognizing that it's only in the tenth week of the tour that he begins to concentrate on getting truly and deeply inside his performance, and closing himself to a degree to what's going on around him, so that he can then concentrate on his work. Up till then he's improvising, and he's improvising off the top of his head, and so he uses devices, tricks, mannerisms – tricks really is the best word for it – he uses a series of tricks to get himself through the parts he hasn't yet deeply felt and resolved.

'A circumstance which is bad for John is when he is working with an unsympathetic director; another is when he is rightly cast and well directed but in a play that isn't right, that isn't going well. Then John's fantastic and highly developed sense of responsibility to an audience is greater than his responsibility to himself and so, of the two integrities, John, unlike a lot of other actors, will sacrifice not only himself but sacrifice the reality of his own work for the sake of not letting down the audience. So that again, where another actor would remorselessly plod forward developing his own role, even if the play is going badly and there are coughs out front, John, the moment he hears a cough, will sense that the house is restless and will produce some brilliant but well-tried stage trick to catch the audience's attention. That's where his great professionalism and his enormous experience are both a virtue and a vice, a manifestation of John's generous and open quality. And in that way it's a great virtue. It is also a vice because in all artistic work there comes a point where only selfishness can carry the artist through to the point he wants to reach. At that point John can easily lose his way.

'Another way in which a director can help John, is concentrating on him more than he would concentrate on himself, creating for John a climate of selfishness that he won't create by himself. So that to direct John you recognize that if you don't intervene till the last day of rehearsal, he will be interested in other people, their scenes, trying things fifty ways and so on. What you do is gradually build a glass wall around him, with an intense spotlight in the middle of it, so gradually, as rehearsals develop, you say "No John, that's none of your business, don't worry about the third act, leave that to the writer. Don't worry about the girl – she's getting on fine", until gradually his sights begin to turn in, despite himself, on his own work. It always has a shedding effect, as it has with all artists, because as their work develops they begin to shed the unimportant to get closer to the essential.'

Working on *Measure for Measure*, both Brook and Gielgud had certain preconceptions, but these were more a springboard than a straitjacket for the work done in rehearsal. Brook says that from the beginning he would have had 'a sense of Angelo, a lot of images, impressions, faces, facets of him, not yet in clear shape. And I'm therefore open to discover, although if someone were to ask me, I'd say "Of course he's in a wild temper here. That's my impression," and I'd be certain that when I start rehearsing this with someone else, that's going to be changed, so I'm not locked at all to that idea. And I then start doing that with John who, because he would have the same feeling, takes this line in which Angelo is clearly in a fury, and would suddenly try it not moving. Now, where another, a different kind of actor would make his suggestion in intellectual terms, and say "Look, I've been thinking of an idea and I think that many impulsive men in moments of great stress are motionless", with John it comes out of instinct in terms of behaviour at the moment, so he wouldn't know why, he would just say "Let's try doing the line motionless". He would just have that smell of something, and doing it motionless, suddenly a line that's apparently a loud, passionate and flamboyant line, will suddenly *isolate*, and at that second, if he is suddenly sensed rightly, you get a clue to Angelo. Suddenly Angelo appears for a moment, and because of that you see him as he could be twenty lines later, in a quite different light. So there, either you or John or both seize on it and say "Ah! But were that true, then we could start quite differently in the following scene". It's a form of impressionism. Once a true detail is found, it gives you a little more light, but the reason you pick that detail and not the other is because you do know ahead – otherwise you wouldn't recognize it. It's this thing of recognition. There is a pre-knowledge, based on study, on turning things over, on trying to define for yourself as much as you can, and John, like me, has that pre-knowledge, and will talk endlessly about it before starting rehearsal. Neither of us will say "Oh we can't talk because we don't know". We have strong theories about it which we'll lay down as law and say "Oh undoubtedly he's this, that and the other". Except that the next day, if anyone says "But you were saying yesterday . . ." we say "Oh, but that was yesterday". But at the time one believes it.'

* * *

It therefore seems slightly surprising that Brook should have
so much liked Gielgud's 1950 *Lear*, which was founded on a
1940 production by Harley Granville-Barker, a director who
knew exactly what he wanted before he went into rehearsal.
'That in fact was one of the most impressive experiences I've
ever had in the theatre. I thought he was absolutely marvellous
and although, years later, when I did *Lear*, I did it quite
differently, I thought at that time if I'd done it with John, I
would have been treating John in that particular experience
the way John was treated by Granville-Barker. I would
have followed him, because it seemed to me to have a ring of
absolute truth and authority.'

Throughout the fifty years of his career, Gielgud has found
no directors with whom he has been more in tune than Brook
and Granville-Barker, who could hardly have been less alike
in their methods of working. But this is Brook's explanation
of the paradox: 'If Granville-Barker gave John everything
from the start and said "The character is like this, that and the
other" – because he was making suggestions which were in
tune with John's general feeling – then I'm sure that on the
first day with Granville-Barker, he gave himself over with the
same relief as with me when I would do that same thing with
him on the last day of rehearsal. And with John – it would be
unthinkable with any other actor – on the last day of rehearsal
very often I would start from the beginning of the play and
say "Now John, that bit you remember where he is serious,
and now it leads through the bridge of this to where he is not
so serious and beginning to laugh" – and give him this pattern.
I would do it on the last day, built out of what we had found
together. But in fact, when the day came, he was only too
pleased to find somebody he trusted telling him, in very clear
terms, a series of things, every one of which he would then
undertake to do because they made sense to him. Now because
Granville-Barker was the only person whose general feeling
and understanding of the play completely coincided with
John's, then John could go towards him feeling that "Whatever
this man says is what I would discover if I worked for three
months on the play". That process happened on the first day,
so when Granville-Barker said "As you come on in *Lear* you
are this and that", John had no wish to argue . . . or simply,
as I said earlier, one sets out towards something and when one

recognizes it, then the process of search is over. I think that with Granville-Barker he recognized immediately that this was right.

'All sorts of roads lead to Rome, and the method of the director being right, the method of the director working everything out ahead of time and then giving it to the actor, is again a perfectly sound method if the director is absolutely right. If I had the capacity, which is alien to my whole nature, to sit at home and think out a play not only completely, which anyone can do, but absolutely unerringly rightly, then there is no reason why they shouldn't. But in fact what happens is that the directors who use that as a method think wrongly and then cling to what they have thought out, because otherwise their authority is challenged, and that's why in most cases it's a bad method. But if a man has the capacity that Granville-Barker clearly had of thinking rightly, he presents simple outlines which the actor can then fill with his own flesh and blood. Because an actor, if he is doing something that is given to him that is right, always clothes it with himself.

'An author writes a role, a Shakespearean role in which every word is rigorously laid down, but the completeness of that structure doesn't take away from the actor's contribution. On the contrary it sucks the actor's individuality into it and that's the same with a director like Granville-Barker. He would be working like the author.

'Today everything is different, all sorts of values being different, ways of work different. In Granville-Barker's day, it was a very much more stable society and therefore a more stable world image. The Shakespearean world as he saw it, and conceived it, in a completely coherent manner, was something that could be given to an actor who shared so many of the same world values as Granville-Barker, in a way that enabled the actor to find it very close to himself.'

Of Brook's five productions with Gielgud, the most revolutionary and the remotest in style from anything Granville-Barker might have done was unquestionably *Oedipus* at the National Theatre. 'The only reason I did *Oedipus* was as a real homage to John. I hadn't worked with him for a long time. In fact I went to Vivien Leigh's memorial service and John read the address, so marvellously and so movingly that this was very much on my mind when out of the blue the

National Theatre asked me to do this *Oedipus*. Reading it I thought "Well, here is the field for a most interesting experiment. This is a play that on the one hand can only be done in terms of group work – that's the only way that the text and its choruses can be realized, and the only people to do this chorus are not chorus people but the very best and brightest and sharpest young actors with the willingness and openness to do the work necessary. And yet this is a play which depends on the word, which to a degree often defeats some of the most interesting actors, who have developed great possibilities of what they call corporal expression, great emotional freedom, but who are eventually at a disadvantage to John for instance when it comes to what he can do so marvellously in his reading." And I thought, here is an opportunity to make a living bridge through work between a whole range of actors. If we all worked together in a particular way, we could evolve a new style for this play that would depend in equal measure on the contributions brought by different schools and would be a product of the two. With that we started on this long series of exercises where the young actors' real appreciation of John was something quite different from what happens when a leading actor rehearses his part and a lot of young actors sit respectfully on the side. John threw himself into the group exercises on exactly the same level. It's equally difficult for everyone but not for one second did it occur to John that he had any special position or privilege. Artistically he was starting from zero and so were the others, and they would attempt the same exercises in the same way. He was always at a disadvantage because a young actor could do physical leaps and turns and twists in a way that obviously he couldn't.

'Then, as the exercises developed and got more advanced, there were things done with great difficulty with the voice and the gesture, and suddenly he would do something so marvellous that other actors who now knew him, not as the John Gielgud of books and photographs but as a man working with them, were acquiring a new admiration and an artistic respect for the fact that he was doing something which they realized was way beyond what they could have found, something that came from the depths of his talent and imagination. Out of that grew a very good relationship and out of *that*, an exchange of influence. And undoubtedly the total level of quality and attitude of speech of all the other actors was affected positively by the presence of John in the company, while John's use of his body and his attempting to use it and relate it to the part were also affected. Because for the first time, his interest and respect for what all the young actors are trying to do was caught in a new way, because he was working with them.'

This phrase 'build a living bridge' is characteristic of Brook and his whole way of working. The director, unlike the painter or the sculptor, is always working with living material, and the moment that matters is the moment of performance, the moment of living contact between actor and audience. This is why he distrusts abstractions, definitions, attempts to impose patterns from outside. At an early rehearsal of *A Midsummer Night's Dream*, an actor asked him 'How can you define what it is that we are looking for?' To questions like that his answer is always the same: that the work done in rehearsal, which goes in a thousand different directions, is always aimed at a definition, but if the definition could be formulated in advance, the work wouldn't be worth attempting.

He does not believe in following a straight line. 'I believe on the contrary that the only way one finds anything is through the radar system of finding one point, two points, three points, and somewhere in between those is what you are looking for. For this reason I've really spent all my working life in looking for opposites, from very early on. If I had worked in Shakespeare, I would then want to do a commercial comedy, if I'd done a commercial comedy I'd want to work in television, and if I'd worked in television I'd want to go to opera. And this to me is a dialectical principle of finding a reality through opposites. So that a line, in a way that can be pinpointed, is to me immediately suspect. So the moment someone suggests "I see, your line is towards ritual theatre" – another totally meaningless label that has been plonked onto a certain type of work – the moment I'm told my work's ritualistic, my instinct is to look for everything in it that is not ritual. And, when I'm told it's not ritualistic, then "ritual" begins to take on a meaning.'

One of his main reasons for wanting to tackle *A Midsummer Night's Dream* was that it constituted such a contrast with everything he had been doing since 1964. 'I find the material I've been working on has taken on a certain gloomy consistency. It's one of the reasons why it seems to me impossible to do even one more piece of work within that key. Because it seems that having worked on the *Marat-Sade*, *US*, *Oedipus*, and a series of *King Lear*s spread over seven years, including years on the film version, it's absolutely essential to go to another part of the world where there is a different form of life enjoyed, as there is in *A Midsummer Night's Dream*. If one's only inside tragic material it's yet another false view of reality. Tragedy isn't total reality, it's a part, a version of reality, not a complete one, and one can't but feel in the end that something is lacking within it. When we did *US* we tried very hard to discover how it was possible to reconcile the horror of a living world situation such as Vietnam with a need to explore it and talk about it through a comic language. A tragic language seemed so woefully inadequate, though in fact the collaborators who worked on it, particularly Albert Hunt, have a very strong social sense and a sense of the relationship of farce to truth. At *US* we were continually moving into burlesque and farce as being perhaps the only way that one can deal with extreme horror. This was much misunderstood by many of the brilliant intellectuals who complained that it was unworthy of a serious theme not to have a certain intellectual seriousness in approach. But we very rapidly discarded that as being more unreal. The sort of academic and serious analysis of the meaning of Vietnam seemed to be farther from its reality than burlesque.'

In some ways each production that Brook has done represents a turning point in his development, but his experimental season at the LAMDA Theatre in 1964 was a particularly important one. With Charles Marowitz as his co-director he was working with a predominantly young group of actors from the Royal Shakespeare Company, devoting a great deal of time to developing a feeling of ensemble through improvisation and acting exercises. He was to go on to work with what remained basically the same group in a private production of Genet's *The Screens* (1964), then in Peter Weiss's *Marat-Sade* (1964) and in *US* (1966).

The title for the LAMDA season – 'Theatre of Cruelty' –
was much misunderstood. 'Although the work itself was presented with a quotation from Artaud* which established absolutely precisely his extraordinary definition of cruelty as being
a form of self-discipline, and therefore cruelty meant cruelty
to oneself. That notwithstanding, for years and years after
that, question after question would be put to one towards
an apparently avowed taste for sadistic material, sadistic relationships with an audience, with actors and so on and so
forth.'

Artaud's hostility to the theatre of words and personal relationships, his interest in ritual, myth and magic, gave Brook
a number of valuable cues for a series of experiments both in
actor-audience and actor-actor relationships. By working intensively with a young group, especially in non-verbal improvisations, Brook found it was possible to create very strong
bonds between members of the ensemble. This was not
altogether a new discovery, though. Already in 1960, working
on the Paris production of Genet's *The Balcony*, he found
that 'Long evenings of very obscene brothel improvisations
served only one purpose, they enabled this hybrid group of
people to come together and begin to find a way of responding directly to each other'. But certainly it was useful in 1964-
66, to do four successive productions with the same group.
Then in 1968, with *Oedipus*, he cut free and used none of the
actors he had used before.

The 'Theatre of Cruelty' season was also a turning point in
that it taught him the value of working with actors over a
longish period without having to produce a polished production as an end-result of the work. An invitation from Jean-
Louis Barrault gave him a chance to create an international
centre of research for actors from different countries under
the auspices of the Theatre des Nations in Paris. The experiment was interrupted by the student rebellion, but in July
1968, at the Roundhouse in London, the group presented a

---

*In *The Theatre and Its Double* (1933) Artaud wrote 'Our long habit of
seeking diversion has made us forget the idea of a serious theatre, which,
overturning all our preconceptions, inspires us with the fiery magnetism
of its images, and acts upon us like a spiritual therapeutic, whose touch
can never be forgotten.

'Everything that acts is a cruelty. It is upon this idea of extreme action,
pushed beyond all limits, that theatre must be rebuilt.'

series of exercises based on *The Tempest*. The actors had reached a stage in their work where they needed the sounding-board that only a live audience could provide, but it was made clear to the public that what it was watching was a workshop. 'We had no sense of obligation to deliver *The Tempest*. Consequently we were free, we could do a *Tempest* in which nine-tenths of the text was inaudible, incomprehensible. This didn't worry us. People who reproached us with that were making a useless reproach. It would have meant many months of work before we could have recovered that same freedom and yet made every word and every line live completely. To do neither thing would have been a horrid half-way house where we would have had to become much stiffer and conventional to deliver the text, or we would have had to say "To hell with the text. This is ruining our newly found freedom. Let's not endanger our freedom. Let the text look after itself." Both of which would have been rotten solutions if the aim had been to present Shakespeare's play. The only good solution would have been to have gone on working month after month to the point where, in presenting the text, we could have found all the freedom there was in the exercises.'

One of the exercises was what Brook calls the mirror exercise. Two actors face each other, one trying to copy every movement the other does as if he were his mirror. This is 'an exercise by which two actors begin to work in harmony. Then four, then six and then eight, and then twelve, until the whole group is working in harmony. This is a basis of working, the product of an actual series of exercises of many different sorts by which the group works very freely together. And this is something that always has to be renewed. The fact that a group worked well last week doesn't mean that it happens this week. It always has to be re-exercised. New problems arise, so that a play can't be approached unless the group is in a good state of preparation.' This particular exercise was not used in the preparation of *A Midsummer Night's Dream*, but, as Brook put it, '*The Tempest* exercises in one way were everything we're doing in the *Dream* or directly related to the *Dream*, which is a pure extension of that work'.

Just as in *Oedipus* Brook had been handicapped by an old-fashioned theatre (the Old Vic) so, in the *Dream* it was a big disadvantage to be preparing the production for the theatre in Stratford-on-Avon. But if Edward Gordon Craig did little work in the theatre because prevailing conditions fell so far short of his ideals, Brook is essentially a realist. 'I have never despised or tried to reject the existing theatre, because it is what it is. Some of it is very poor, and some of it is very good, and some is a mixture of the two, but it exists. And as long as it exists, it is a requirement that has to be fulfilled. Now Stratford and part of the Administration exist in dramatic forms that are criticized very strongly within the directorate. It exists for instance in buildings that I dislike. I think the Aldwych is an awful theatre, and this Stratford theatre, which changed its name to the Royal Shakespeare Theatre, but still remains the Stratford Memorial Theatre, built by a lady who knew nothing about theatres and approved by a committee of local worthies who knew nothing about theatre, has been amended and amended by a series of directors over the years, but it still is not the theatre that is needed for playing Shakespeare. The acoustics are really poor and Shakespeare of all things demands sensitive speech. The first requirement of a Shakespeare theatre is an acoustic miracle in which actors can play freely and lightly in a warm living way, so that the colours that they bring to the words are very rich. If you have to play Shakespeare in a cruel theatre, where, if you don't face front and speak at a certain pitch, at many points you can't be heard, then you're in an instrument which, by its very nature, introduces tension into playing and precludes a great number of qualities that a much more relaxed playing produces.

Now Peter Hall has tried to change this situation by using enormous initiative in getting the Barbican; 'one day we may hope that someone will set fire for a second time to the Stratford-on-Avon theatre and it'll be rebuilt.* It is inadequate and can't fulfil the needs of a group trying to present Shakespeare because it doesn't correspond with what any of my colleagues really needs. But it exists. It would be woefully inadequate and irresponsible to say "So we abandon it." We have to do as best we can with what are still the best conditions that exist in the world at this moment for putting on Shakespeare – which are the possibilities given by this imperfect but evolving organism called the Royal Shakespeare Company.

*The original theatre, built in 1879, was destroyed by fire in 1926. The new theatre, designed by Elizabeth Scott, was completed in 1932.

'*A Midsummer Night's Dream* has to happen within the context of this theatre. Now that means that I cannot think of *A Midsummer Night's Dream* within the context of the Roundhouse. While on the other hand my own work and the experiments which have been evolved are such that I cannot for one second believe that the type of proscenium theatre we work in with a thousand people sitting in fixed rows staring at the stage is in any way right for a modern audience.

'I feel this is completely out of date, not only as a fashion but out of date since it isn't a living relationship that really would make the most vital acts of theatre happen. I tried to do this in *Oedipus*, and *Oedipus* was an experiment which took us about as far as we could go in struggling against a given requirement, which was the architecture of the Old Vic Theatre. We tried to turn that into a virtue by encircling the audience with actors strapped to pillars. The sort of thing which would have been very natural at the Roundhouse was here a fight to the death against the building. In Stratford, to build platforms all over the auditorium, consequently cutting the one thousand seats down to five hundred would make it neither fish nor fowl. It would not be the Roundhouse, it's not the sort of work we could do in many other places. So the whole way of thinking has to be in a sense amended. But not the aim, because there's only one aim in any theatre work, and that is to reach a living event, a living experience; it is the means that have to alter. To make a living experience in one architecture demands quite different means from another.

'But it's like the difference between one play and the other. The moment you change plays or you change subject, all means anyway have to change. To me the continuity is always the same – trying to discover how a living event is made. You can make a living event by improvisations, without any material and a living event with existing materials may be quite different and in many cases more intense. When you deal with Shakespeare, the intensity of the material gives you the possibility of reaching an infinitely higher level of vitality in the event than could be achieved without that marvellous material.

'It's always the same problem – unimportant whether it's comedy or tragedy – how can you close the triangle between subject matter, the performers and audience? It's always the same task – three points that have to be linked. And always the problem's reopened because given conditions are always totally different. In this case the given conditions mean that a lot of what we did in the Roundhouse cannot possibly be applied directly, stuck on that stage. And yet other things can be applied very intensively but apparently indirectly.'

Rehearsing the *Dream*, Brook started with a lot of exercises. In the way he now works, this always comes first. Second comes the understanding of the play – not an intellectual understanding but a translation of the printed text into living terms. 'When you have a play which is poetic and subtle to a degree, you can't achieve collective understanding – everybody understanding what they're playing – by the director making a speech, as a sort of pedagogue who has worked out what he thinks the play's about and then explains it to his actors. Eventually the quality of the result depends on a shared understanding, not on one man's view. For an actor to go on a stage with conviction, conviction that really carries to an audience, he has to know what he is talking about, and to know what he is talking about, he has to believe, and to believe means that he has to be inwardly committed. If an actor is given a point of view which he finds plausible but which he doesn't deeply feel, he may try his best to commit himself to it but it would be very different from the commitment of an actor who has really shared in the discovery. The actor who is trying to sell to an audience an idea or an emotion that he really isn't sold on himself feels shifty. But an actor who's representing something that he knows and has experienced and can defend as his own truth, has no embarrassment about presenting it. Quite on the contrary, he wishes this to be known.

'This is an enormous long way to go when you start with any subject. In the case of *US*, on the first day we gathered our actors together and said "Now what does everyone believe about the war in Vietnam?" And thirty opposing views arose, most of which were very vague, ill-informed and unformed. Three months later there was still a diversity, but the subject had been lived with, and the people who took one side or another took it with passionate conviction, because they had learnt their way into the subject. And when we had open debates afterwards, the actors each spoke very individually about what they felt.

'And in the same way, you start with the *Dream*. It's far from Vietnam, but a play with the greatest subtlety and mystery. But before a director and a group can find any forms by which this can be presented to the public, we have to explore, we have to learn for ourselves by first-hand experience what this play is about. Where somebody studying *The Tempest* in a library uses intellectual and analytical methods to try to discover what it is about, actors try to discover through the voice, through the body, through passion, through involvement, through experiment in action. And in that way, by trial and error and elaboration and rejection, the themes of the play become clear as they come to light, become visible. So the process of rehearsing a play like the *Dream* is very simple. You can read the play together two or three times and then it becomes boring. Soon you feel that first-hand experience is needed. In the case of the *Marat-Sade*, the first-hand experience we needed being about madness, for days we could use the true living material of each of the actors, who almost all had had an encounter with madness. The madness was either in his family, amongst his friends or in himself. So for days we could put aside the text and pour out together experience that related to it. Whereas with the *Dream* people don't come with the same amount of material on spirit life that they have on madness. According to statistics, three-quarters of the families in the world have madness in them, so it's instantly available. But you can't do a play about the spirit kingdom if the actors think it's just a lot of old shit. Well, you get a group of people and say "What do fairies mean to you?" No good answers will come out of that. And until you get past that stage you can't start working on *A Midsummer Night's Dream*. How can you get past it? Experience from everybody's life? "Has anybody here seen a madman?" Everyone says "Yes", "I know one", "I am one." "Anyone seen a fairy?" "No." "Are you a fairy?" Blushes, confusion. Right, one voice saying "Well, maybe". The only first-hand experience you can then get is trying to explore the text and that means using all the specific acting methods of which the work done in public on the Roundhouse *Tempest* was a partial reflection. That is the sort of thing which, when done by actors, and then examined and discussed by them all together, brings the play out in the open.

'For instance you can achieve exact relationships. In the case of *The Tempest*, the Japanese actor – by approaching Ariel through his breathing and through his body – made Ariel something very understandable. A certain force became completely tangible in something which to the Japanese would be easy to understand because it was the basis of the Noh theatre from which he came; he brought a certain type of sound, a certain type of cry, a certain type of breath. The idea of a force was truly represented, and so it could be discussed, it had suddenly happened – there it was amongst us. It was no longer "force", an abstract word, it was a reality, something that could influence another person. Now in the same way improvisations, amongst other things, can through a long process of time, begin to give one starting points from which to uncover the many worlds of the *Dream*, the interweaving levels of reality, the reality of Bottom, his world . . . What is this reality? What reality is it contrasted to in others? What reality is this contrasted to in the fairies? These vague and theoretical terms gradually become precise and clear to everybody, because everybody has gone through the same explorations together. But when, after a sufficient series of practical experiences, you come back to discussion and find the terms of reference have become stronger and clearer through work done, work shared, you begin to have a conviction which is your starting point. Through this come, right at the end of the line, the physical means and the imagery.

'In the case of a Shakespearean play, it is difficult to bring that freely discovered raw material into perfect harmony with a text that is absolutely set and can't be changed in any way. At this point there's always a nightmare period, because the discipline of a text is very hard to swallow. The moment the actor tries to concentrate totally on the requirements of the text, a lot of his freedom disappears. It's not his fault. It's completely out of his control. He respects the text and wishes to master it, but as long as the difficulties aren't completely overcome, one is corseted, imprisoned within the requirements which are always fantastically difficult in Shakespeare. Shakespeare has the same terrible difficulty that Mozart holds for singers: there is no mercy, no indulgence, it has to be totally mastered. There is a long period when the efforts to master the discipline involve a total lack of that very freedom which gives the life and the richness to any performance. No, either one comes through this stage or one doesn't.

'Very early on in rehearsal, the actors did a free improvisation on *A Midsummer Night's Dream* and I think of all the many years I've been connected with improvisations this was far the most thrilling piece of joyous lunatic surrealistic free theatre I've ever known. It was a performance for just those of us who were there in rehearsal, completely off the cuff and from which energy burst out and made something quite memorable, a fantastic piece of collective invention. Everything that was in the rehearsal hall was somehow pressed into service and there was something like . . . the end of the *Marat-Sade* when the whole asylum went berserk and wrecked the place. When we made the film, this scene was so genuine that it lasted three hours and the actors wrecked and set fire to the set at Pinewood, and we filmed it over the three hours. It was a great happening and there was this joyous release after playing that constricting, cramping film, to feel it was the end. And everything really went mad. In exactly the same way there was an explosion of energy in the *Dream* cast that expressed itself in the most staggering invention. At the end of it one had been present at a real theatrical event, an event in the sense that it could never have been repeated. What we had gained from our work was a marvellous feeling of excitement amongst everyone who had participated in it, and a number of lights thrown on many parts of the play, just by pure inspiration of the moment. But the moment all the energy went on to working the text naturally, there was no longer any energy left for this sort of spontaneous life, and so we had to go into a stiff and rigid period.'

As in the work on the 'Theatre of Cruelty' and on *The Tempest*, a point came where a sounding-board was needed. 'The rehearsal process is something that in theory is all private until the first night. In fact the ebb and flow is more complex, and there comes a point when the existence of an audience, if the audience isn't destructive, crystallizes certain things, reveals certain things – in other words presents a challenge and a searchlight which enables you to take the work a good step farther. Now half way through the rehearsals, already something incestuous has come into being for the cast. The cast is too at home and in tune with itself, and its locked doors and closed walls. If there is an outsider there, already something for better or for worse emerges. That's why I've always felt that it's not possible to do experimental work without going out on a limb and exposing it, when we know that we are not ready. That's why for instance at LAMDA, nobody at the time could follow why we did a lot of exercises whose meanings at the time was considered incomprehensible. Only when people saw the *Marat-Sade* two years later did they see the relationship between them. But for us it was vital. It would have been masturbatory to have worked and worked and never taken the challenge of exposure and confrontation that there is, because then you realize where you're on a totally wrong track, where something is a genuine disaster, and you can bluff yourself for years if you don't face that awful moment of seeing that it's no good at all.

'Now in the same way in our work here, in the middle of rehearsals and three-quarters of the way through, one needs that confrontation. At the same time one is dealing with the most sensitive thing there is, which is human material, and everybody from actors to director is at this point very raw and very vulnerable and very susceptible, and one can be destroyed by a harsh and negative judgment. So that to show our work to critical adults could be purely destructive. That's why we were saying that the perfect audience for our purpose is an audience that has great attention and that has no judgments in the adult sense of the word, has a direct interest judgment, but not the sort of adult judgment that is really withering and paralysing for a sensitive actor. It's got to be quite different, it's not to be critical in that dangerous sense of the word. And at the same time, children are a generous audience and a very, very demanding audience. So you can't do bad work for children, you have to do work at your best. Probably they were the audience we needed.'

In most productions of the *Dream*, the fairies, the nobility and the artisans seem to constitute three separate worlds but, as Brook saw the play, they were 'three very intertwined and overlapping worlds. It's a play about worlds within worlds; it's not for nothing that it's a play about a play about a play.

Because one sees that these hard and fast divisions are just first level definitions and that the more you get into it, the more they evaporate and melt. For instance the same actor is playing Theseus and Oberon, the same actress is playing Hippolyta and Titania, and the same actor is playing Puck and Philostrate.'

He was also conscious of Shakespeare's very deliberate use of alternation between verse and prose. 'Bottom and the mechanicals speak in prose and it seems to me a clear starting point that the mechanicals are in a prose world which in Shakespeare always suggests that one has to look outward. The verse world is a world in which one must look inwards into the text, in the sense that it's a concentration of the meaning and that one can't start by a feeling that one has to embroider. Through the verse one must look into the intention: the moment that Shakespeare is writing in prose, it's almost as though there's an obligation to develop, as you would for instance a modern realistic play.

'The prose passages demand that turning into flesh and blood existence for which realistic elements have to be found and in *A Midsummer Night's Dream* the prose portions suggest a social context. The working men are putting on a play, which, if you carry it through quite simply, compels you to reconsider from scratch the place of Pyramus and Thisby. If you once imagine in terms of social reality a group of artisans attempting – because they believe in it passionately – to put on a romantic play, it seems obvious to think that the comedy should lie in laughing at unqualified people doing something badly. Are the mistakes of illiterate people funny, or is this a rather unpleasant upper-class tradition? And in fact I wouldn't even call it upper-class – a sort of middle-class tradition. Because the upper-classes and aristocracy have always had a much more generous attitude, like the Duke himself, who says very clearly in one of the most eloquent speeches of the play that when he sees a man stammering and shivering and blushing in front of him, he perceives his intention and doesn't find anything to laugh at in his mistakes and embarrassment and sweating palms. And here Shakespeare gives one of his major speeches to expressing a theme which cannot but throw light on a major portion of a play, which I think too easily is considered funny without the nature of that fun being really evaluated. Because if one once starts from a fellow feeling for the hard attempts of non-intellectual people to break into an imaginative world with love and respect and devotion, with their own untutored efforts, the play of Pyramus and Thisby at once takes off in a different direction. This is not interpretation but a direction dictated by a realism, which is called for by a prose world. And in the same way that the Stanislavski question of "What is Oberon doing in the wings?" is silly, the Stanislavski question of "What is Bottom or what is Snug doing?" is as pertinent as it is in Chekhov. And that is why in Shakespeare I have always maintained that there is not one style, there is not one method. That the glory of Shakespeare is the co-existence of a thousand opposites which in practical terms demand a thousand opposed and contradictory approaches to co-exist within one performance.

'I keep on saying to the cast – nothing is by accident in Shakespeare. Nothing can be explained away as the conventions of the time or "Oh well he did it because he didn't know what to do, or he wasn't thinking that . . ." If you come rigorously back to this, everything becomes a very difficult question to answer. "Why did Shakespeare, writing in the full flood of his talent, put Pyramus and Thisby in the key position?" The play could end without this last act, entirely. The whole of the story wraps up when dawn comes and the lovers are reconciled, and were it a Mozart opera, there you'd have your final sextet and go home. And he writes a last act that is apparently in dramatic narrative or neat comedy terms, totally superfluous.

'You can say one of two things. You can either take a camp and fruitless view which is to say "Well he wrapped his plot up by the end of Act Four and sat down to think what the hell am I going to do? And reached for a new idea". Or you can say he is a conscious writer, who knows what he's doing, when he puts the play-within-the-play in the star position at the end of the end and makes a whole act round it – an act that begins with a long and apparently gratuitous speech about the poet and about imagination – again not necessary. This is such a strong intention of Shakespeare's that one has to revise one's views of the entire play, asking what necessitates this and no other form of the last act. And why is it that the play in fact couldn't exist, couldn't have its meaning without this?

And the moment you open that question, once again the relation of Pyramus and Thisby to the Duke and lovers changes.

'The first production I did in this theatre was *Love's Labour's Lost*, and I did it by just the same premiss of saying nothing can be by accident. Therefore what can it mean – the entrance of Mercado at the end of the play? After a two and a half hour pastoral lyrical comedy without a single dark thought in it, suddenly death enters in the last reel. This seemed so fantastic an event that one couldn't not take it as a major intention. And I'd seen the play performed, I think, once upon a time, and had been amazed to see that this – as it had no place in comedy – was treated rather lightly, so as not to intrude too much. It seemed on the contrary that it was there as an intrusion, and we played it and rehearsed it and explored it as an event, a world-shattering event. And in fact, having done so, it amended one's feeling about the balance of the whole play. The taste of the play was totally changed by this artificial world having put up against it something very different – this reality intruding at the last moment. Even if it was an early play, it was not there for nothing. The whole play found its proper resonance in this dark moment at the end.

'It's the same process of thought that makes one say "If this is so clearly intentional, then all the lines, the curious jokes of the Duke, the odd difficult lines that come through the lovers' interventions – all need to be appraised very carefully". In *Love's Labour's Lost* the entrance of death at the end doesn't change your interpretation of anything that preceeds it, because it is a gratuitous act right out of the blue, like the killing of Cordelia in *Lear* suddenly as a thunderbolt that falls donk onto the play. It's not made inevitable by things that happen earlier. It's a twist.

'In *A Midsummer Night's Dream* when Hippolyta says "This is the silliest stuff that ever I heard", the Duke makes this marvellous statement about the whole pretentions of theatre. From our point of view, the difference between rotten acting and superb acting seems to be enormous. It's the bottom and top of the mountain. From a different point of view it's not all that important. What is important is not only what the actor is doing or what level the actor achieves, but what the spectator brings; the actor is searching for meaning that is only completed with the full, active co-operation and complicity of the spectator. Theseus says that depending on what we bring to it, the quality of what the mechanicals do can be made or marred, and that if our imagination enters in the right way into their efforts, they may pass for excellent men. Many things are said through this last scene which makes what we are speaking of much easier to define – clumsy people doing a bad play badly, noble people being poetic and brilliant, spirits being not as easy as all that; it is much more complex and in another way much simpler. Because they must say how that line echoes back to a line that again is not there for nothing. Not that Shakespeare didn't drop pearls of wisdom from time to time when he felt inclined, but in the middle of a farcically comic scene, when the mechanicals are rehearsing, they go through the whole history of the theatre, of what illusion is. The whole of Brecht's life's work is contained in the argument of whether you represent something by *being* it or by a token, like a man saying he's a wall. And at a certain moment, talking about the Lion, Bottom advises how to make a lion in a Brechtian sense, so that he presents Lion without there being any element of excessive emotion or involvement of the audience. Not only should he clearly say "I'm not the Lion but Snug the Joiner", but he adds this further line "Because I am a man as other men are". Now, if you relate that line which sings out of the text (although it's not meant to be a line suddenly delivered like "Oh what a piece of work is man") to the Duke's: "If we think no worse of them than they of themselves, they shall pass for excellent men", and you tie that to twenty other lines in different portions of the play, then a whole new scale of meaning begins to come out into the light.'

Any attempt to describe Brook's way of working, whether in his own words or not, is inevitably incomplete. Any description of what he gets actors to do with their bodies and their voices can be only partially successful. In *Oedipus*, for instance he worked for three weeks with the whole cast before showing any of them a script, and even if someone had kept a detailed log-book of rehearsals, it could tell only part of the truth about the exercises and experiments, about the strenuous physical and and psychological gymnastics or about the efforts he made to teach the actors to resonate from their chests after playing them records of Tibetan monks.

But this summing up would be more incomplete than necessary if I ended it without trying to give some impression of what the experience of working with him is like from the actor's point of view, and what effect it can have on an actor's development. Invariably, like psycho-analysis, the process is painful. And it goes without saying that there are some actors who maintain that the pain is unnecessary, that equally good results can be achieved without making them suffer. Others have found that they have gained insights into areas of their own reality which no other director could have given them.

The English actor, more than the Russian, the American, the Italian, the Japanese, generally feels inhibited about displaying raw emotion. One of the main virtues of English acting is its restraint, its coolness, its freedom from demonstrative self-indulgence, but one of the major disadvantages of that restraint is the filtering effect it has on the discharge of libidinal force, which often needs to be present during the creation of a characterization, even if it is only present in performance as a foundation, invisible to the audience. Without being entirely neutralized or entirely censored, these libidinal elements are sometimes tamed more than they ought to be, not by the director, but by the actor himself, though with the director's unspoken – perhaps unconsidered – acquiescence.

One actor who was talking to me about Brook used the word 'cruel', but immediately added 'I think he has to be. That's the way he has to work. I mean he doesn't leave you any options. You either resist and you get nothing out of it, or you lay yourself open, and have some fairly punishing rehearsals. I don't mean he's saying awful things or putting you down, but you feel that he's metaphorically trying to tear you, really tear something down there.'

Nearly all actors feel that there is a more savage side to their natures than usually gets shown in performance. They may be aware, when they sit in an audience and watch a great actor like Olivier, that part of his magnetism and of the excitement he generates depends on the feeling he gives of animal power which could be unleashed at any moment. But being aware of this is very different from being able to throw off the inhibitions that usually hold these dangerous-seeming forces in check. English acting is less restricted today than it was twenty years ago by the middle-class tradition of gentility and good manners, but most actors have an inherent resistance to displaying facets of their own personality which might strike an audience as unlikable. And beyond this understandable anxiety there are barriers that can be broken down only with the help of a good director. Probably none of our directors has been of more help to actors in this way than Peter Brook.

To take just one example, Ronald Pickup, who gave an excellent performance as the messenger in *Oedipus* who has to describe how the King blinded himself, told me how much Brook had helped him by telling him to rehearse the speech as if he were a gargoyle, a kind of monster. 'Just envisage yourself as a strange shape off a Gothic cathedral or a monster out of a voodoo ceremony, or something like that.' Pickup then rehearsed the speech in a much more grotesque way than it could be played in public. 'I was using the text, but he said "Feel free about warping words". The word *stand* didn't have to sound like *stand*. One could do anything with any of the series of words, but one was really concentrating on sound from back beyond the time words were invented. Just having the words vaguely sitting on top of it. I remember that exercise most vividly because I think that was the time when I felt it really broke through. And the most ugly, awful – but for that speech real and right – sounds were coming out. And then, as time went on, it was possible to integrate them. I also went through a period when I used to do it very statically, right from the beginning. And then it started to go a bit dead. And only some two or three days before we opened, he said "Forget all that business about coming forward and just doing it there. Do it in slow-motion, glazed time, as if you'd been stunned by what you've seen. Or if you want a naturalistic image, think of it being like a watchman, ringing a bell, announcing the news, going along the streets, telling it to the waiting population." So out of that came the thing of sludging through blood. Which also gave it more weight – because I'm a very lightweight actor. It made me feel more weighty than I'd ever felt before – heavier, in a good way.'

Peter Brook can even influence actors who have never worked with him. John Wood, who did not join the Royal Shakespeare Company until the *Dream* was in the repertoire found that it altered his whole conception of how an actor should be working. 'It's something to do with reaching back and down into the pre-history of which the language spoken on the stage is the Modern Times. You sat in the audience at the *Dream* and if enough of the actors and the audience were in the right frame of mind, the sensation was of being one of a circle of people where the actor-audience relationship as it usually is disappeared. One seemed to be part of a circle of people celebrating something or observing some ceremony. Religious words are perhaps the right words to use. It seemed to me that we all experienced and celebrated the terrible dark agonizing contradictions and horrors that forced Shakespeare to write *A Midsummer Night's Dream*. What we seemed to see was the lowest and farthest tentacles of the roots of a tree of which the foliage is the words.

'It was to me an extraordinarily opening experience. I admired very greatly what the actors were doing, the dazzling displays of skill which were then immediately revealed as mere skill, and denied. I think somehow we should all be doing that now. I think that actors should look at themselves in relation to the character that they are to play, not in the terms in which that entity is different from other people but in the terms in which it's the same as other people.'

PAUL SCOFIELD

❦

The actor Peter Brook has used more than any other is Paul Scofield, who has been in eleven of his productions. At Birmingham Rep in 1945, Barry Jackson bravely entrusted the twenty-year-old director with *Man and Superman*, followed (after it had turned out successfully) by *King John* and *The Lady from the Sea*, and in these three productions, Scofield, who was then twenty-three, played John Tanner, the Bastard and Dr Wangel. In Brook's 1946 *Love's Labour's Lost* at Stratford-on-Avon he was the fantastical Spaniard, Don Adriano de Armado, and in the following season's *Romeo and Juliet* Brook cast him as Mercutio. In *Ring Round the Moon* in 1950 he played both twins and in *Venice Preserv'd* (1953) he was Pierre to Gielgud's Jaffier. Then in his season with Brook at the Phoenix in 1955-6 he played Hamlet, the Priest in *The Power and the Glory* and Harry in Eliot's *The Family Reunion*. He was also Brook's Lear, starting in 1962 and returning to the characterization in the film seven years later.

Like Gielgud, he finds that being directed by Brook is quite a different experience from working with anyone else. 'Yes, I think that whenever I work with Peter I find myself, as you say, in a completely different category. But I have worked more for Peter than I have for anybody else and we worked together so very much at the beginning of our careers, that it's probably less true of me than it is of John Gielgud. Because I think Peter's influence is perhaps more alien to John – by which I don't mean that I have resisted it in any way – than it is to me. I grew up with Peter, and John was very much in a strong and developed area of his own before Peter ever entered it, whereas I was completely raw material when I first worked with him. But I think that while I do, as it were, switch on to a different wavelength with Peter, it's only because of my long association with him. I work in exactly the same way with him as I do with anyone else. I don't change my responses, although I feel much more at home with him.'

The extent to which he was influenced by Brook is not easy to assess, partly because they were so young when they started working together. 'At that time he had no specific method that he was following in the sense that he has now. So that if one worked with him now for the first time, one would have to find that one was being influenced by Peter as to method, as to the way of working. But his influence in the early days was simply much more through contact with a very acute, perceptive, imaginative approach towards the plays. In a way working with him was quite traumatic. One was suddenly thrown up against a directorial influence which was so demanding of whatever intellectual powers one possessed – which were so undeveloped – that I suddenly found that the business of being an actor was something quite different from what I had perceived, even as a student.

'I think that hitherto I had been fairly preoccupied with training my equipment, as it were, and relying on my imagination and on what I fondly considered was my intuitive sense of observation about people. Peter made me *think*, which is something quite different, and think in relation to the play as a whole, and the part that the character took in the general pattern of what the author was assembling. But this was actually quite a natural piece of education for me because I was very young at the time, and perhaps if it hadn't happened through Peter it would have happened through somebody else. But it literally shocked one out of any sense of complacency one might have had, and when one is very young and learning a profession, one feels most complacent, I think. Not that one knows everything, but that one's confidence has never been assailed. The more one learns about such work as we do in the theatre, the less one can feel sure of oneself.

'And at this point I encountered Peter and he was the kind of person who delivers shocks to the system, not by calculation, but just by confrontation with his intelligence.'

Even then he must have had more sense of the whole than most directors?

'Yes, he did, he did absolutely. He would have a conception of the play at the first reading which to us, at the Birmingham Repertory Theatre, seemed almost impertinent. That anyone so young should presume such grasp. And being a tight-knit group, as every repertory theatre is, we would resent this and we would feel "I don't believe this assumption of grasp". But not for very long. This was the first defensive reaction to the impact of Peter. But it then took perhaps two days for us to realize that his grasp was fully backed up. This was quite a salutary shock to us. I for one was simply aware that I was working with a director who could use what I had to offer but not indulge me at all. I was growing and developing and I suppose I was showing some signs of having resources and reserves, and he probably recognized this, but was very very disciplinarian about it. He didn't ever tell me that I was marvellous. On the contrary, I think he detected a certain laziness in me and tried to correct it.'

So you had a feeling that he was making you use more of yourself?

'Yes, absolutely. Whether he was really interested in doing this or whether this was just the thing that was natural for him in order to get the play that he wanted, whether at that time he was interested in the art of the actor, I don't know. But certainly you could feel him becoming a director of actors rather than simply a director of a play. Actors were perhaps at that time becoming to him very clearly instruments that he could draw from – not manipulate, but use in the best sense.'

The voice Scofield uses in conversation is quite different from any you remember from his performances. 'Well I suppose it bears very little relation really to what I do on the stage. Or it seems to. Probably I've never quite used the voice that I speak with in everyday life. But then who does? One has to expand in order to enlarge one's voice in order to be heard. It's difficult to describe because I have no system. With every play that I do I try to start absolutely from scratch, so that I will begin rehearsal in a very neutral way, vocally. It isn't a hit or miss thing so much, it's a question of the voice growing out of what becomes apparent to me about the kind of man I'm pretending to be. It's possible that I may begin to feel like him in my face or in the way that I sit down, or in the way that I walk, before I come to sounding like him. Or it can be the other way. There may be just one line in the middle of the second act, say, and suddenly it will become clear to me that this is the way for this particular man to say that line and this is the kind of voice that emerges from that understanding. That's the beginning and then everything begins to match up to that tiny piece of insight.

'I think it's nearly always the voice which leads me – and I think a lot of actors – towards other characteristics of the person one pretends to be. And I think the reason it's the voice is that it's the spoken thought which is given to us by the writer. I mean it's his, the spoken thought that he has asked us to pass on to the audience. This is why it's nearly always the most important thing to feel that your voice is responding to what he's written in a way that makes sense. Other things follow, things that you hadn't planned to do at all, simply because they're the sort of things you'd do if you were speaking in that sort of voice.'

Sometimes this leads to a voice which is quite outlandish, as in *Expresso Bongo*. 'I suppose that was an approximation of my reaction towards people I have come across that lived in that kind of agents' world. And by agents I'm not talking of agents that I have worked with professionally, because theatre agents are very different. I'm talking about a kind of agent – the pop singer's agent – that in fact I haven't very much experience of. In fact I've hardly met the people in that world at all. But it doesn't take much to find the parallels in people one does know.

'Though it's a fairly dangerous way of working, because one only has oneself as a source of reference and what one's ears tell one one's own voice is doing, and when one hears one's voice played back on a record, it's a great big surprise. So that it's easy to see why one can be very much disagreed with. What I, for instance feel is the right voice for a particular character, perhaps makes other people think "I don't understand at all. What does he mean by that voice?" Things sound differently to people. Not only does my voice sound different to you from the way it sounds to me, but it would sound different again to someone else.'

This explains something about the way he sinks himself into a character. He does not erase himself, but he is never tempted to use the role as a vehicle for putting his own personality across to the audience. Without being physically protean like Alec Guinness, or a virtuoso with greasepaint and nose-putty like Olivier, he disappears into the role, changing his gestures and gait to fit the character, creating shapes which stay in the mind long afterwards – his narrow, lightweight, mincing Khlestakov in *The Government Inspector*, his broad, bearish Macbeth, his gaunt, gawky, angular Vanya, his square, earthy Lear.

Sometimes the process by which he creates these shapes is touched off by the costume, as happened with Khlestakov. 'The walk and the way I moved was very much dictated by the costume, and I think this is not to be underestimated. One's movement is immensely influenced by a period of costume. But while I was most interested in finding the right voice for that, I never really saw Khlestakov as looking like anything I could put my finger on, or sounding like anything that would make me think "Oh that's what I would like to sound like". I was much more interested in finding in him the means of expressing everything that I knew about pretensions. Because this was a kind of definitive representative of pretension in literature. That character just becomes intoxicated by the success of his pretensions – and also by drink. But this is a lovely, a joyous thing to try and do. Because pretensions are funny, and one observes them so often in a censorious and distasteful way. It's rather nice to be able to put them to good use and be able to make comedy out of them. It wasn't so much a person, because Khlestakov is in a way not really a person. But he represents so much foolishness in us all. That's what I loved.

'I was simply interested in making that kind of behaviour true, whatever kind of person one was being. It probably broadened the character quite a lot. It probably made him pretty unbelievable in a sense. But I do that more and more. I find myself being much more interested in finding in a character something which is common to a lot of people.* I believe that when a writer creates a character of any sort of dimension, he is not specifying how he should look, how he should walk, exactly how he should be, but that he is a kind of person that we can all recognize and find some of ourselves in, see a lot of people that we know – friends – find things you have contact with all the time in life, and make these things clear through the means of the character, not in any sense approximating to human characteristics but by being

*Compare John Wood's remark on p. 59.

64

absolutely specific. When one thinks for instance of Tolstoy and the kind of characters that he portrayed, he is pretty specific about the way he describes people, but one finds so many people one knows within his characters. But I feel drawn to attempting by means of acting what maybe a painter attempts. I can see in a way that my attitude to acting has changed very much. I become less and less interested in myself in performance and much more interested in what the writer has opened up for me and how I can best illustrate this, almost without feeling that I am present.'

This is not the way most actors function; nor did Scofield start off by functioning like this. He is very clear about the point of arrival at this change of objective. 'The turning point is very precise in my mind: it was when I did a play called *The Power and the Glory* with Peter Brook. It was a whole new experience, because that was a very muddled play – I suppose necessarily so because it was from a very episodic book, and if they had attempted to make a neat play of it much of the wandering feeling would have gone, the kind of nomad quality that the character has, and the kind of contact with all sorts of people. And so this very diffused structure of the play allowed me in a way to wander with it and to find a kind of freedom from not being too bound by precision. Technical precision certainly is a very good thing to learn, but perhaps I found at that point that effective acting was not what I wanted to do. That I didn't want to make effects. But I wanted, as it were, to leave an impression of a particular kind of human being, or create an atmosphere in a scene which an audience would take or leave, to a certain extent, as it wanted to. Not be too definite, not say "This is what this person's like, this is this kind of man, this is what the story means".'

Leaving things open rather than closing them.

'Yes, but it was mostly for me as an experience of liberation in finding myself free, finding that within the security of the character I was playing, I could do anything. It was interesting – it didn't matter what I did. It was like improvising in a sense except that I'm not an actor who could improvise without a script.'

And I wonder whether that's got something to do with a desire for a particular kind of contact with an audience, saying

'*Here are the common factors between the character and you*'.

'I think so. Because I have a much greater sense of contact with audiences now than I used to have. In fact the contact one has is a very mysterious one. It's absolutely un-analysable, and you can talk about the sense of whether the audience is listening or not, whether they are concentrating or not, whether they're coughing, whether they're laughing, the satisfaction you get from the laughter and the degree of intensity of their concentration and all these things. None of that is very satisfying, but there is one thing that always interests me very much. When actors are in rehearsal, the director takes the place of the audience completely. He becomes the focal receiving point for everything one is doing, every attempt one is making to clarify the play in terms of acting. And then, when the play gets in front of an audience, the feeling is in fact exactly the same as if one were playing to one person. The director has removed himself and because he is not there one is only aware of his influence through what one is doing. But an audience feels like one person, and I have no possible explanation of that except that I think there is something very mysterious that happens to people when they're en masse – a greater or smaller mass – and are concentrating all on the same thing. They have in common what they're watching, but they also contribute to each other in a curious way. And the feeling at the end of the first act, and the feeling at the end of the play from an audience is quite different from when the curtain lifts up. Something unifying happens.'

But he also focuses his awareness on the space. 'I'm always aware of the four corners of the theatre in terms of my own vision. If I'm not, then I think it's fairly clear that they're not going to be aware of what's going on with me. I don't mean I'm thinking about those people, but aware, within my field of vision, of their existence, so that I don't miss anybody, so that there isn't a completely forgotten area that hasn't come within my peripheral vision. In films of course I think unconsciously one is still doing it for an audience. That is, one's still thinking in terms of the consumption of what one's saying and thinking, although they're not there.'

Certain roles, obviously, provide more opportunity than others for the kind of contact with an audience that Scofield now wants. There is a Vanya in every member of the audience, so *Uncle Vanya* provides more opportunity than Osborne's *Hotel in Amsterdam*. 'Yes, very much more because *Hotel in Amsterdam* is essentially a very claustrophobic kind of idea. The whole play is concerned with the obsession of a group of people about one other person at a particular time of crisis, and going round and round this man and this moment of rejection of him. Which is such a very restrictive piece of geography in a sense, one couldn't get away from that central idea at all, so that was really what was important in the play. And it was quite interesting that the character himself was a man who didn't appear. My character was obsessed by him. He in a way was the most interesting character in the play, although he didn't appear. He was a kind of Diaghilev. It might have been the way Nijinsky felt about Diaghilev. He was necessary to the others, but they wanted to feel they could do without him. It's quite a common relationship, I think, not only in the art fraternity but amongst people who employ people. That was interesting about that play. But *Vanya* opens up an enormously wide field of comment about waste and guilt and guilt *about* waste. It says it so beautifully. And it doesn't say anything – that's what's so extraordinary. None of the characters are specifically articulate about the sense of waste they have inside them. Underneath all the commonplaces it's all there. Chekhov was able to choose virtually quite fatuous things for people to say and to indicate beneath them what they are really thinking about.'

Anna Calder-Marshall, who was Sonia in the Royal Court production of *Vanya* described what it was like to find herself playing most of her important scenes with Scofield. 'It takes such a load off acting when the people you're with are just *there*, and they change from night to night and you realize you couldn't do a speech in the same way, because you're getting different things all the time. Some nights I was a bit too soft. It's very difficult at the end because it can be sentimental. One night I was indulgent and I felt I wasn't helping Paul enough. The balance between the two is very delicate.'

Scofield, in turn, praises her capacity for responding freshly each evening and each moment to the impulses given to her. 'She's an immensely flexible actress in that way and I think it's because she has got a mind, and she relates and reacts extraordinarily to the person she's working with. Which is why she would find what she found, working with me. I do like to establish a very free kind of open relationship so that things can be changed on the impulse of the moment. The tone that comes from somebody else, that you never heard them do before, can absolutely radically change your feeling about the next thing that you have to say, and you just allow it to. She's very open to suggestion in this way. She's really there. She has the intellect to grasp the moment of a change like that if something is happening. She can use it and take it over from there. I found her quite remarkable. She has a very strong feeling, but she senses when it's exaggerated or false or unnecessary or redundant. And when an expression of feeling would be one which would do what the audience should be doing. Sometimes one must hold back feeling, otherwise the audience is not going to feel it. I think one must hold it back very very strongly, because what one is trying to represent as the feelings of a character very easily becomes infused with one's own personal sense of sympathy with the predicament, and the audience then sympathizes less.'

I suppose particularly with somebody like Vanya who is so sorry for himself.

'Exactly, and that's all one must show. Not how right he is to feel sorry for himself. Or what a shame it is. They're two separate things, the expression of what Vanya feels and the complete holding back of what *you* feel. You can only arrive at the expression of what Vanya feels by means of your own feelings, so that in a way a kind of split has to happen. Or by means of your own understanding of his feelings, your own perception. In order to see clearly one has to be able to feel as well. But then I think one has to make a very very clear division and not allow one's own feelings to intrude. It's impossible of course to stop them altogether. But at the same time one has to make the effort. It's like crying too much and then audiences don't cry.'

Of course there ought to be nothing unusual about the flexibility and the sensitivity that Anna Calder-Marshall has

in common with Scofield, or the ability to respond to whatever happens on stage, to create a new set of variations in each
performance which slot in with the variations that are occur-
ring in other people's performances. But in fact this kind of
spontaneous creativeness is not often found. 'It is very rare.
Oddly enough it seems to be a facility that people lose as they
get successful. That's a great generalization, because there are
some who've got beyond that and through the rocky, shaky
time of early success, when either the actor settles for repeating success or is determined to press through to possible non-
success, simply in order to grow. And some do do that. But
what I think I am trying to say is that usually you find this
amongst actors who are beginning – you find this sensitivity
to impressions and to influences from the people they're working with, so that there's something reciprocal going on all
the time. But when a certain amount of success is achieved,
then for safety's sake people are inclined to stand still and try
to repeat whatever it was that worked last time. I think this
does something which closes the mind to response. Because
it's only by being willing to start again every time after
whatever it is that you've done, whether it's worked or
whether it hasn't worked, whether it's been considered successful or not, it's only by starting absolutely as if that had never
happened that one can remain open to influences from other
people.'

Scofield tries never to repeat himself and never even to
repeat the same method of approach. His intention is to start
on each new characterization without preconceptions, to go
to the first rehearsal of each production without knowing how
he is going to set about working. 'Sometimes things happen
very fast and sometimes one has to take one's time. I'm very
careful not to let any kind of pattern emerge too soon. I also
learn a lot from other people when I'm working with them.
If I'm very sure early on of what I want the final result to
be, then I can sense that quite soon. Of course it happens more
often that one isn't sure. But sometimes it happens I am. I
was very sure right from the beginning of *Government
Inspector*. I knew what it should be almost from the first
reading, and I was right – whether it was good or bad I don't
know, but it worked.'

Many actors are already thinking about effects they want

to make in performance before they even go into rehearsal. But just as a director like Brook will devote the early part of a rehearsal period to digging into the material without planning how any discoveries will be used, so will an actor like Scofield. 'I find that energy in rehearsal, the early part of it, has got to be devoted entirely to thinking, and that my equipment – my voice, and what I'm doing, sitting, standing, or whatever – has got to be completely in abeyance, forgotten about, lost. I don't waste any energy on that because I don't yet know what I'm doing with them, so I must leave them to be idle and get on with it up here. It's only gradually and in the last stages of rehearsal that one can use the kind of physical energy that is needed in a performance, because then the whole man, as it were, of the character is functioning along the right lines.'

If actors can be divided according to whether their prevailing interest is in style or in accuracy, Scofield's is unequivocally in accuracy. 'I'm not drawn towards expression of any sort of beauty in the theatre, beauty of line or movement or voice or anything.' In a Shakespearean part he would never give priority to speaking the verse as verse. When he played Macbeth in Peter Hall's production at Stratford-on-Avon in 1967, he started by breaking the verse up into very short phrases with pauses between them that seemed arbitrary and became rather distracting. But by the end of the run at the Aldwych (April 1968) he had settled down into a far steadier reading of the part, breaking the natural rhythms only in the 'Tomorrow and tomorrow and tomorrow' speech, where the staccato he introduced served both to make it seem less of a set piece and to illustrate the disintegration in Macbeth's mind. The broken rhythm in Scofield's speaking reflected the changes that had overtaken Macbeth's capacity to think in a straight line.

'With words like those, that carry so many strong tunes with them, you have to fight to find the freshness of them. And you have to make them *yours* in some way. And I'm prepared for it to sound ugly as long as it has a kind of fresh meaning. Of course I would rather do justice to the poetry than do that, but if I found myself speaking the poetry beautifully, or getting near to doing so, or in any way being preoccupied with speaking the poetry beautifully, and found that

70

it was not really alive, I would rather sacrifice the verse. Because one's going to lack something somewhere. I don't imagine that a performance of mine of Macbeth can have all its aspects filled in. And I would rather miss that kind of perfection, in order to aim for something that was recognizable as the truth about that play, in a fresh way. Not fresh for the sake of being fresh, or fresh for the sake of being original, but just in order to make people hear it as if for the first time.'

Working on *Lear* with Brook, Scofield had found that his performance, like the production as a whole, always seemed to have existed in embryo from the beginning of rehearsals. 'It grew, and there was a lot of very very hard work done on it, but there was nothing that had to be scrapped.'

Whereas in Macbeth you had to recognize false starts and make radical changes in approach during rehearsal work?

'Yes, it was very much more difficult, that. I never had a very clear sense of the wholeness of the play. I grasped the play, in a sense, in my mind, but I never felt the end of it at the beginning of it. I, as it were, stepped from ice floe to ice floe, with a great sense of insecurity and danger, but that was my fault. I never somehow succeeded in making a whole character.'

Scofield does not feel that he fits easily into roles calling for military characteristics. Most actors have difficulty with the warrior aspect of Macbeth: Scofield had difficulties too, but there was no sign of them in the performance. 'Maybe if it worked it was because I paid great attention to it. Because I thought perhaps it wouldn't come too naturally. It was a most fascinating and elusive affair, the character. I don't feel I've done it yet. I want to try and get it. It felt really quite passionate, but I can quite believe it didn't really look it. Perhaps it never really emerged.'

I thought it was more passionate at the end of the run.

'Well I think so, I think it had grown, and I think we had grown through a lot of difficulties. Which is always a rather exciting thing to happen, because if one does find the hiccough at the initial stages of the opening performance, it's very exciting when the actors themselves, through working together, eventually work through to finding a kind of unity. I think it was perhaps unity that it lacked. But how a particular group will react to a particular play can never be predicted, especially one of the huge plays like that.'

In *Hamlet* there is the same problem of bringing the meaning freshly to life theatrically. 'It's hard to keep away the mechanical processes of taught interpretation, however freshly one tries to think about it. Probably the first time I played Hamlet, I had something of this problem, and I didn't really resolve it the second time I played it either. It was maybe fresher the first time. It was the second time that was more difficult and the problems of the play became more painful in a way, more painfully difficult to try to solve. I found myself almost out of sympathy with the character, and I found that the dominant note of revenge, of vendetta as it were, that's in the play, is something which doesn't really communicate to modern audiences. That you seem to be "carrying on" a great deal. In Sicily perhaps it might strike a more immediate response, but one has to work very hard at that to make an audience sympathize with a planned revenge. So that he seems to be very self-absorbed, in fact, and that's not what Shakespeare intended at all. What must have been impressive to the audience when it was first done was the family sense, the sense of family pride and the absolute need to avenge his father, which I think eludes a modern audience.'

Scofield is open-minded about the advantages and disadvantages of working in permanent companies like the RSC and the National. In any case, as he says, there is no long-standing tradition of ensemble theatre in this country. 'I think the Moscow Art Theatre, for instance, work in a very different way from the English. They seem to work together for so long that any sense of staleness in their relationship has been long passed and they seem to have developed a very strong, extra-sensory awareness of each other that binds them all together and makes them able to anticipate each other. I think that companies like that are used by their directors in a most remarkable way. I think that they cast actors not in any kind of conventional way, saying it's the right sort of person with the right sort of voice. Because they know their actors so well they know their sympathies, they know the amount of insight an actor has, whether an actor's understanding of human nature can penetrate that area that Chekhov has written. They seem to explore each other a great deal in that way. I suppose we in our permanent companies have not been together long enough.'

In his first appearance at the National, as Voigt in *The Captain from Köpenick*, Scofield had a great opportunity of finding common factors between the character and the audience. 'He seems to represent almost anyone that's ever suffered from bureaucratic restrictions and the kind of callousness that was so very well represented in Gian Carlo Menotti's *The Consul*—people waiting in offices and people ignoring them. And this terrible wearing down of the morale, especially of people who don't have the money and the influence to go swiftly through the bureaucratic barriers, but who are kept waiting on the outside. I suppose this is something that I feel very much in sympathy with and indeed I can't imagine who doesn't. But it's rather nice to have a specific means of expressing the kind of distaste one feels for that kind of officialdom and the kind of advantage that officialdom takes.

'I suppose it can very easily be explained in terms of people wanting power but I think that's a little bit easy – I think probably fewer people want power than one imagines. But it's a complete insensitivity to other people I think mostly, that makes certain types of officials behave in a very cruel way to supplicants, to petitioners, to people just simply wanting a pass, or a passport, or something signed, or something stamped. They're made to feel very small, and are made to wait.

'Of course he's a very particular case, this character, because he's not just the Patient Citizen. He's in fact somebody who has overstepped the bounds of law and has been in prison. He's an old lag, as it were, but a very minor one, a very petty one, someone who simply forged a postal order when he was very young and who got an enormous and very savage prison sentence for it, and when he came out, found it very difficult to go straight again, and did something else minor and went back in again. You know, it was a rut that was impossible to get out of. So in rather a pallid and negative creature, some kind of violence was growing out of a simple human rejection of this kind of treatment. So there is a specific point in the play which is very sentimental – the death of the girl which seems to be what sparks him off into a kind of violent defiance of the powers that be. And from then on it seems he has no doubt. That something very positive must be done before he dies.

So that the means of getting his passport, which is what has been denied him all these years, becomes also a kind of moment of assertion of his own living – that he will do something to be remembered, to be noticed at least.'

I wonder to what extent this kind of consideration is either a conscious or unconscious influence on your choice of parts.

'I can't say that it's conscious because I can't say that I choose such and such a play because of the relevance of its content. One might say it's unconscious but I do consciously – I won't say choose or pick – feel sufficiently drawn towards it to say this is something I would like to do. A kind of human predicament that I recognize, and maybe that I think "Well, I understand that sufficiently to be able to do it justice". And then it becomes exciting because it is something that you can see a clear line of action through.'

But this could work equally with a figure who represented a viewpoint antipathetic to your own?

'Yes, it could, very very easily. It gives one a kind of inner satisfaction if what the character is about and what the play is about is something about which you also feel quite strongly. But it wouldn't make any difference if it were running counter to that current because it would be equally interesting to find what is sympathetic – not necessarily sympathetic because sympathy doesn't matter, but to find an understanding of a viewpoint that one doesn't share.'

The vocal range and flexibility Scofield has developed are enormous. Voigt, Lear, Thomas More in *A Man for All Seasons*, Vanya, Johnny in *Expresso Bongo*, Khlestakov, and Charles Dyer in *Staircase* all spoke in remarkably different voices. 'I had a certain vocal range at the beginning, although I didn't know how to use it, and consequently I was inclined to stick to one area vocally. But I think it was in the first place a conscious effort when I was learning to be an actor, the actually conscious effort of making myself go as far as I could in every possible direction, and being in a way rather foolhardy and believing that there wasn't any area that I couldn't go to, although that sounds very immodest. I don't mean that I necessarily thought I could do anything. But I thought that I could try. And particularly perhaps in rep. and at Stratford-on-Avon where one was given a wide variety of parts in a short period of time, so that simply to exercise myself I suppose I must have consciously tried to extend my range. But, even then, for a long time, I didn't succeed. I mean there's always an area of range that one just doesn't have anyway. But I went to the first rehearsal of *Venice Preserv'd*, which was directed by Peter Brook, and I did Pierre and at the first reading I saw the possibilities of the character, but something seemed totally missing somewhere in terms of myself doing it. And Peter said to me after that reading "Of course you do know that you're going to have to find a new voice for this". And I went away and thought about it, and I really consciously, almost for the first time in my life, *consciously* decided on a voice, decided on a specific timbre and depth, and during rehearsal set about trying to get it. And I think in the end that I did. I at least know I changed my voice for that part, and felt that it worked, and that was the first time really I ever knew that that was what I'd done. Apart from obvious characterizations, like playing old men, I changed my voice in this instance in order to be able to encompass an area of emotion and a kind of man who was still my own age but different from me. I was quite young at the time and it was a very vigorous character of my age, but my voice wouldn't do. It wasn't right. So I had to find another. And this taught me it was possible. But I haven't since then consciously done this. I haven't since then made this my aim – to change my voice – it's only been necessary for me in order to express what I feel is in a character.'

But I suppose once consciously having done it, unconsciously you go further than you otherwise would.

'Yes, exactly. One is aware of the kind of limit one can try, and so one tries even further than that.'

Macbeth is not his only performance to have grown very substantially during the run. His empirical method of working, his flexibility and his honesty make this kind of growth not at all uncommon. Even his Sir Thomas More in Robert Bolt's *A Man for All Seasons* – one of his most famous performances – had by no means fully matured when the curtain went up on the first night. 'Of the things that I've done, this was perhaps the least well represented at the opening. We hadn't found a way of doing the play, and I know I was very muted. I think that I was kind of hovering in the wings as it were, wondering how to play it. The tentativeness was simply because I couldn't see where I must commit myself.

'The voice on that was indeed a great problem to me, because the strength of conviction involved in that character was such that there was one point at rehearsal when I was sounding like Tamburlaine the Great or something. Because by putting that amount of strength, literally, vocally, one became kind of a booming, bellowing hot-gospeller, just simply trying to put the full force into the man's convictions. This was clearly quite wrong, and what was missing was the total discipline and restraint of the man, and it was possibly at that point that we opened. And then there was much too much discipline and restraint, though in the end I found a balance.

'And I suppose I attempted to interpret the kind of legal way of thinking of the man in terms of a sort of dryness. This may have in its initial stages been a little too dry. I think that possibly the only way to arrive at the right kind of voice for Thomas More was through the way he thought, which was as a man of law. And a man of law doesn't necessarily speak in a dry and restrained way, but that's a way to find it. And then the humanity of More will be added to it and the appetite for life which he had will be added to that and finally one arrives at all the colours being there in the voice.'

What was it like transferring that to the screen?

'It was very exciting, because I think for the first time I felt that I knew what I was doing in a film. And this was only because I had a large knowledge of the play and the character, and was not starting from scratch and was able to meet the technical demands of film-making, which I was comparatively new to, with a predigested knowledge from beginning to end, a sense of the development of the man, of the story, of the whole thing. So that wherever I was shunted to in the picture – I mean one day one might be doing a scene towards the end of the film before one had been through the development which led to the man's being in that particular state – for the first time this was not a worry to me, because I had it all inside me. I could switch from place to place, although in fact Fred Zinnemann who directed it didn't do that very much. He shot it to a remarkable extent in continuity.'

Without being in any doubt that he has learnt a certain amount from films and television that has been useful on the stage, he is sure that he has gained more from his work on the radio. 'It's not just the question of vocal effect, it's a question of absolutely truthful thought, which if it's not there on the radio is very apparent. And I suppose in the same way, working in front of a camera does make you simply think in a totally concentrated way. But I think one has to think in a totally concentrated way in the theatre. I suppose it's possible not to, without it showing too much. But if you *do* use that kind of concentration in the theatre, that shows.'

But of course concentration is only one of the elements necessary to an effective performance. Ever since he played Henry V at Stratford-on-Avon in his first season there, he has been 'terribly aware of the kind of energy that was needed in a large theatre like that. The theatre in those days seemed larger than it is now, because the stage was further back because of the orchestra pit and one seemed very isolated from the audience. It seemed like an immense effort to communicate at all. It's a much better theatre now. And this of course is a lesson that all actors have to learn at some time. It is extraordinary how, when energy is not being consciously expended, a performance dies. And I think that you have to come to learn this, and I think it's quite hard to learn – that you can't just sit back and think and be true. One has to generate and push through one a constant current of energy, through what you're saying and doing. Even on the evenings one is tired, one must. In fact what I think an actor very often finds is that this current of energy comes through more strongly when he is tired, because it's not springing from any natural vitalities, it's having to be forced through tiredness.'

However much a performance varies in other ways, the supply of energy must remain the same. 'When a performance changes by emphases and shifts, by means of spontaneous thinking – because one is thinking freshly and differently, one hopes, all the time – emphases do change, and I think this can only be sustained if the energy is constant. It varies during the course of the play in that some moments of a play are more relaxed than others, but relaxation doesn't mean a cessation of energy.'

One of the qualities that distinguishes the really creative actor from actors who are merely competent and effective is his ability to keep himself and his performance in a state where freshness, spontaneity and invention are always possible. This is easier, naturally, when he is working in a repertoire. 'With one play on Tuesday and Wednesday and another on Thursday and Friday the two plays mainly benefit from this because one comes very very freshly from one play to another. In a long run in the commercial theatre, it's possible to keep spontaneity, but it's very hard work because I think the human mind does reject repetition, and there comes a point when it can just say no and refuses to remember. And you don't remember, and that's very frightening. That's the extreme result, but in between spontaneity and that refusal of memory, is a whole area of a fight against being mechanical in any way – being mechanical because you cannot bring your mind freshly to exactly the same thing every night, night after night, for twelve months.'

But an actor can also make too many sacrifices for the sake of working in repertoire and become stale by staying too long in a company like the National or the RSC. Scofield has done stints with both. 'But I don't like to feel that the theatre is divided into very sharply segregated fields in which you can only work in that bit. After all, the English theatre itself has its boundaries. It's not a vast and limitless field and I think it should be explored by an actor in every area.'

For an actor like Scofield, as for any real artist, the right to explore freely is indispensable. He is essentially an actor – one with no driving urge to direct and none at all to have a company of his own. Indubitably he is making more of a contribution to the English theatre by keeping himself free than he would by tying himself down to any institution.

TERRY HANDS

One of the oddities of the present situation in the English theatre is that while it is reaching out with some success, towards more popular forms, the directors who have given it most help to engage a wider audience are university graduates. Earlier on, in the ten years after the war, Joan Littlewood, who was working-class by birth and anti-intellectual by disposition, tried in vain to create a working-class theatre. The audiences that flocked to her productions in the East End came from West London. But our theatre today is far less exclusively middle-class. Working-class elements have been incorporated not only into the audience but into the acting profession and into the substance of the plays. At the same time theatre has become more socially conscious and production style (which has been influenced by Brecht) aims not only at articulating the social sub-text of a play but at communicating more directly with the new audience.

The theatre which did more than any other to bring about the change was the Royal Court under George Devine, who started not from any social or political premiss but with the intention of giving the writer a better deal than he was then getting in the West End. At the same time he hoped to engage better writers. This idea of writer's theatre was based on the sort of respect for literary values which a university encourages. Devine has been President of Oxford University Dramatic Society and nearly all the directors he collected around him at the Court were graduates of Oxford or Cambridge – Tony Richardson, William Gaskill, Lindsay Anderson, Anthony Page. The Court served largely as a model for the RSC and the National, both of which were mainly dominated by graduates. Kenneth Tynan, the policy-forming scarlet eminence of the National, was an Oxford graduate and nearly all the Associate Directors of the RSC are graduates: Peter Brook had been at Oxford, Peter Hall, John Barton, Trevor Nunn, David Jones and Ronald Bryden, the RSC's Play Adviser, were at Cambridge. Terry Hands had been at Birmingham University.

The argument is still sometimes put forward that the universities are a bad training ground for directors, that instead of becoming familiar with methods of theatrical communication they learn to fall in love with ideas for their own sake. The alternative argument is that while certain ideas cannot conceivably be translated into theatrical effects, a director's job is to co-ordinate actors and effects to communicate with an audience, and the more alert he is to the ideas that are bubbling through the play and the social and cultural ferment he is living in, the more likely he is to be able to involve an audience in what he does with a play. This would certainly seem to be true of Terry Hands.

Like Peter Brook, Peter Hall and Trevor Nunn, he rocketed to the top of the profession while still in his twenties. At twenty-three he was running a Liverpool theatre he had started himself, together with two friends. Two years later he was put in charge of the RSC's Theatregoround. The day after his first full-scale production for the RSC, *The Criminals* by the Cuban playwright José Triana (1967) Peter Hall made him an Associate Director. He was still only thirty-one in 1972 when he became the first foreigner ever to direct a production at the Comédie Française, where his *Richard III*, with Robert Hirsch, was one of their greatest triumphs for the last twenty years. The two most important formative experiences were reading English Literature at Birmingham University and working in a non-proscenium theatre at Liverpool. At Birmingham he learnt the value of close analysis in preparing a text; at Liverpool, working almost without scenery on a thrust stage and needing to make each production as different as possible from the last one, he learnt how a theatrical space can be filled with just actors and costumes.

The seminal idea behind his theatrical career was to start a graduates' theatre. 'Occasionally we competed in the National Union of Students' Drama Festivals and we talked with other people from university theatre groups. We had a dream. Perhaps one day we might start a little graduates' theatre.' When he graduated, though, he would have preferred to carry on as an academic. 'When I left university, I went to RADA – not because I particularly wanted to go into the theatre. I was more interested in doing research, but I was advised not to by my tutor, John Russell Brown.' He wanted, at all events, to go on having something to do with literature, as he would in the theatre. 'And the first test was getting into RADA. While there I began thinking more about starting my own group. I met Martin Jenkins, from Liverpool University, who was working for the Royal Shakespeare Company. We decided to try and start a theatre. We asked Peter James to join us. He had been at Birmingham University with me and then went on to the Bristol University Drama Department. I tackled the Equity side and the business of setting up a company, Martin found the venue, the theatre. It was Christmas 1963 when we actually decided to go ahead. I left RADA and we were open with a couple of shows by 28th September 1964. So in all it was done in about nine months.

'We started on ten pounds a week for everyone except the fireman, who had twelve pounds ten shillings. He was older. Our friends were there. Some were students, some were RADA actors, some were from Bristol Old Vic Theatre School. We had general auditions in Bristol, Liverpool and London. We took a company up. We rehearsed well and opened, appallingly, with *Henry IV Part I*. There was a beat group in a cellar. We could only play three evenings a week, so we had to play five matinees – which is one of the reasons we started to think of schools audiences. We built the stage and put the seats in with the help of the university students. We bought timber off demolition sites. It was all very adventurous – like boy scouts setting up camp. But we were making a theatre.

'None of us had done very much direction. I'd done one production at university, and a mime play at RADA. Peter had done more, so had Martin. We learnt as we went along. We began as a triumvirate. Shortly after opening Martin became ill and had to leave so I took over as the Artistic Director. Then, when I joined the RSC, Peter stayed on and ran it till he went to the Young Vic. We had some interesting actors: Cyd Hayman, Tony Pedley, Philip Manikum, Stephanie Beacham, Bruce Myers, Hildegard Neil, Terry Taplin, David Bailey, John McEnery and Susan Fleetwood. Alan Dossor is now running it and has already managed to double the audience we had.

'It was incredibly hard hours and unhealthy conditions, and a budget for a show was fifteen pounds. But it wasn't all as difficult as it appeared. We had no set to speak of, so fifteen pounds was enough really. The scenery didn't matter, it was the actors. And in a way it was the most marvellous training one could possibly have had. In proscenium theatres you've got to have scenery, because the focus of the arch is on the air, it's between the stage and the ceiling. It's a gap, and it needs scenery to direct the focus onto the actor. With the thrust stage, the focus is on the stage, so provided you've got a stage, you don't need anything else on it except an actor, and perhaps something for him to sit on.

'When I was in Liverpool, Bolton wanted its own theatre – which it now has. I can remember Blackburn wanting its own theatre; someone there said " I've got two cinemas and I'd love to have one of them converted into a theatre". I think any young directors today, if they really want to learn their job, could go up to these places where there is no theatre and get going. It only needs approaching people in the right way with the right determination.'

Unwittingly, Terry Hands was equipping himself with the ideal background of hard experience for the job he was going to do with Theatregoround. In Liverpool, building up an audience out of nothing, he was proving that there was a potential demand for serious theatre. 'We had to find a new audience. The Playhouse was taking the whole of one type of audience. The Royal Court was still going there then, and that was taking the Number One touring dates. There was also the Empire, which usually ran a spectacular of some kind. Outside London, Liverpool must be almost the only city in the British Isles which has four theatres – we were the fourth and coming in at the deep end. We went for younger people, fourteen or fifteen to about twenty-five. We wanted a popular theatre which would speak simply and emotionally. Not academic theatre or necessarily escapist. Altogether the programme was fairly bold. We got very few people in if we did Arrabal, and a lot if we did Beckett. Peter James's production of *Waiting for Godot* was I think our most popular show. So the choice of plays wasn't altogether wayward and it wasn't altogether unsuccessful. We had a very good Board of Governors, very understanding and concerned with theatre. They only once demanded a pot-boiler. We did *Rattle of a Simple Man*. It had the worst box office of the season.

'I felt I ought to leave after two years. I'd used up anything I could think of, and I needed to learn. It seemed to me if I stayed any longer I would simply be repeating what I'd known before I came to Liverpool, without actually having had the opportunity to go out and gain new experience, because the workload was so heavy. So I asked my agent to write to the National Theatre and the Royal Shakespeare Company to see whether they would take on an assistant director. The National wrote back a very polite letter saying they were full and the Royal Shakespeare Company wrote back and said come and have an interview. And I had an interview with Michael Kustow, who at that time was looking after the RSC Club, and then I saw Peter Hall. He asked me to start Theatregoround.

'I was given *carte blanche* – Peter simply said " Providing you break even, I don't want to know. Get on with it". So we did. By Christmas we were doing twelve performances a week, and in the first week of January we did seventeen and the week after sixteen. We had about nine shows on by that time : a version of *US*, Chekhov's *The Proposal* done in four different styles, a version of the *Shepherds' Play*, three anthology programmes, *An Actor at Work*, which was a demonstration programme, and so on. The pressures just got too much, so we cut down and started operating more sensibly. At the end of 1967 we held a three-week season of Theatregoround work in London at the Aldwych – anthologies in the morning, demonstrations in the afternoon, and shows in the evening.' One of these anthology programmes Terry Hands compiled himself under the title *Pleasure and Repentance*. Describing it as 'a light-hearted look at love' he used songs and texts from mixed sources including Sir Walter Raleigh, Micky Spillane, Tennyson, the Rolling Stones, Prévert and the Bible.

Productions were taken anywhere. Working in halls, clubs, community centres and schools all over the country, the actors gained valuable experience of working in different spaces, under different conditions, striking up lively reciprocal relationships with very different audiences. Performances which looked as though they were aimed at bringing culture to the masses would have met, naturally, with hostility, but by playing to school-children in the afternoons and then, in the evenings, to parents who had heard enthusiastic accounts of the show, the company made contact with many people who had never seen Shakespeare in performance.

'We found the moment we were prepared to come and play in their own halls, people were grateful. And so were we. We learned about our audiences – we began to learn what people wanted. Which was theatre of all kinds. I don't think theatre's dying. It seems to be growing. Perhaps a certain kind of theatre is dying. But the theatre of "They're doing a job and their job is to communicate and our job is to be communicated to" seems to be growing. I don't believe that television has affected theatre that much. It has siphoned off a lot of naturalistic plays, thank God, and it may have killed music halls. In general it seemed to be encouraging theatre-going.

'We tried to make friends. I don't think you can proselytize in the theatre. You can only make yourself available. Perhaps you can do something to break down prejudices – get rid of some of the suspicion. Whether it is the audience that dresses up in its best clothes and treats you like royalty, or the audience of Hammersmith kids who tell you to piss off.'

Promoted from Theatregoround to work on full-scale productions for the Aldwych and Stratford-on-Avon, Terry Hands found himself uncramped by any conscious or unconscious pressure to conform to a house style. 'The Berliner Ensemble has a clearly marked house style. I don't think we have. All the directors work independently and differently. We share the same economic limitations and the same author. Shakespeare is the most difficult playwright in every possible way, not just for directors, but for actors too. If they can do Shakespeare they can do anything. Shakespeare constantly stretches not only the apprehension of the actor, his ability to grasp extraordinary thoughts, but also his equipment, emotional and physical. Shakespeare seems to specialize in the extraordinary, the amazing rather than the mundane.

'If you work fairly constantly on plays like his, with the focus so much on human beings and their potential, obviously some kind of approach develops, and this may be something we share. Clearly we share certain beliefs, certain ideas, or we wouldn't be in the same place. But as far as that becoming a style – no – I don't think so. Personally I work differently on every show – a different preparation, a different approach to rehearsals. On *Pericles* we did about two or three hours of improvization a day, emotional and physical. Textual work came later. Everything was very free. With *The Merry Wives of Windsor* our concern had to be sociological. The concentration was on village life, trying to recall all those things that make for a happy country life, like warm fires and porridge and things of that kind. Most directors, I would have thought, do the same. Trevor used improvization for *The Shrew*, not for *Much Ado*. It's entirely to do with the show. There's little similarity between Peter Brook's *Lear* and Peter Brook's *Midsummer Night's Dream*.'

But if the RSC productions are compared, broadly, with National Theatre productions, certain differences emerge, which do not derive simply from the fact that the RSC virtually has Shakespeare as a resident dramatist. It has more resident directors and fewer guest directors. There is therefore more continuity of approach. It is not easy to define this, but as Terry Hands says, 'It is an approach which perhaps spends a bit more time purely on the actor, perhaps a little less time on what surrounds the actor.' Here again his experience of working on a thrust stage at Liverpool was an excellent preparation.

'As all our work at Stratford is concerned initially with communicating Shakespeare's plays, obviously we must become aware not only of what he appears to be thinking but what kind of people he was observing and how they might have expressed themselves. The problem with the actors of today is that they're already influenced by the centuries which have come in between and have set up around themselves a whole system of rules of expression and limitations on expression. If the Shakespearean line they have to say is a peculiarly happy line, they will search within the social and fashionable milieu of today for what *kind* of character would say it and how he would say it. It isn't just a man being happy. For instance, the twentieth century has been very much influenced by two world wars. Either we go with the military influence – we have the stiff upper lip, we don't say too much, we're highly self-disciplined – or we react against it and go to the other extreme. What we don't have is the simple individual means of expression Shakespeare had. The country was thinly populated then and there was space in which any kind of individuality could be expressed freely.

'We work in two ways with an actor: first *from* the line to suggest the motivation, and then we do a tremendous amount of work to make sure the expression is very free – at least initially, so that it can be shaped by the characterization later. With a naturalistic play the characters are usually described at the beginning, and whatever the actor says is governed by the rules of being a bank clerk or being a hairdresser or whatever he is. The way he stands, looks, speaks, is limited by imitation of somebody's behaviour patterns. This seems to me the worst way of acting.

'With Shakespeare one looks for the motivation and the freedom of expression without yet having recourse to the modes of today, though of course we're bound to be influenced by them. Shakespeare's plays seem to be a great celebration of individuality, of eccentricity, of what is extraordinary in human beings, not what is ordinary. So the next thing is to help the actor into a position where he can simply express himself, whether it's purely through the lines or through a sound or through his body. We have a movement director who works on all the productions at Stratford, a voice director who helps them vocally on each production. And we also work on the sonnets, the idea being that if the whole focus of communication is going to be achieved through the actor, the actor must be free, physically and emotionally to express the motivation, the moment it comes to him, simply, and quite freely without thinking.

'For the company therefore we tend to look for actors who are not highly equipped technically. High technical equipment always tends to be in the fashions of yesteryear. We look for someone who is in himself a bursting or a riveting personality. The expression and the logic of what he's doing will then be organized by the ensemble.

'As a director I'd never dream of "blocking". I haven't done it for many years. The production will end up the way it will end up, but the actors will end up that way because they have needed that amount of physical movement to express what they wanted to express. The actual form of positions and shapes on the stage is unimportant. That can normally be done at the last minute.

'So in terms of Shakespeare's verse one says "Yes, the verse is your friend, the verse is simpler than prose. It shows you where to breathe, it gives you a rhythm, a rhythm of expression. But that is only a conduit, a gully, for the content, which comes from that original impetus, if only it's freely expressed. Until it's freely expressed, rehearsals cannot proceed. The only use I can see for improvization is not to use other words, because they bring other problems, but to find improvizations of expression – whether through singing, through chanting, through noise, through howling, or through a physical position – then the line will become just the punctuations of that emotional response. An enormous amount of Shakespeare is onomatopoeic. It can be understood by people who don't understand English.

'The blank verse system is so free and so marvellously alive. And secondly one must try and make oneself like an Elizabethan to the extent that one is prepared to feel an emotion and seek for the means to express it – to express it verbally. Nowadays we do tend to generalize our emotions – if we're angry we kick the wall or throw something or swear, and the words we use are very general – alliterative but general. What seems to be clear both in the courtly writing of the Elizabethan period and indeed the language as it's reported to us of what we'd call the lower orders – the beggars or whatever – seems to have been more precise, more lurid but precise. So that anger – though it may end in blows, it may end in death – goes through a stage where someone really wishes to describe the object or person that's annoying him. It's like any other acting process – you feel the emotion or the motivation or the impact, and the desire is not to *do* but to speak. Working on that takes time. The reason we tend to generalize our emotions nowadays is that most actors tend to think of what to do rather than what to say. Freedom of expression needs to be encouraged. We are told that in Shakespeare's time Englishmen used to laugh and cry a lot. They were lovers of loud noises and bright clothes. So one comes to an actor and one says "You can apprehend the thought first, but then feel it, and then *want* to speak". It's like the treatment of a soliloquy – we don't do them in inverted commas or "He's alone in his study". It's simply on the assumption that in going into a soliloquy nearly all Shakespeare's characters say "Now I am alone" or "Thank goodness they've gone," or words to that effect. And there's always that sense of urgency, the need to speak. A soliloquy always seems to begin, in *Hamlet* for example, from an actor playing the scene and then getting rid of the others just so he can come down to the audience and say "Look I'm alone now. Now I can talk to you".

'I don't believe audiences are in the least bit interested in what an actor is feeling on the stage. I think they only care about what he makes *them* feel. Often it's an unconscious process. Hence the need for them to seek an outlet for their emotions in words. But if you go to some student plays, and you see an actor sweating and dominating the stage and suffering deep emotions, it doesn't mean a thing. But the moment he turns to you and makes *you* feel it he's sharing his problems – he says "To be or not to be, that is the question". As though *you* have now got to argue out in your mind whether to commit suicide; it seems to me only then do you become involved in the dilemma. That's why a lot of our work is towards persuading or helping or encouraging the actor to do that.'

If there is a Royal Shakespeare Company house style, then, it derives from an effort 'to put the language first, but to try to support it. Our work is half textual and half physical. The better the actor, the less you need scenery. When things are going badly with the actors, the solution is always bung on more scenery. It normally saves the day, patches up the cracks. We have been accused of a house style in our scenic approach more than in anything else. We've experimented with white boxes. But then there aren't many ways you can tackle a proscenium arch, and boxes have been used before. We became very much concerned with the space in which the actor worked and the light that hit him in that space. The more space we could give him, and the more light, the better he seemed to be able to do his job. It also creates a much greater dynamic. For instance, ask an actor simply to convey that he is *thinking* on stage. If he's sitting down, you'll find he can do it by any number of means. He can start to play with something, or he runs his fingers down the edge of his chair, or he sways, or swings. If he's surrounded by scenery, all the energy of that actor in fact is going into an object. If you take away all those things and leave him standing there with nothing and you say "Think", he nearly always has to do it by some type of movement. He begin to move and it starts to register in his whole body. The whole energy of the thought is then available to the whole audience. It's not going into an object. This makes a great deal of difference. I haven't had any furniture in shows for a long time. There was one throne in *Richard III*, nothing else. *Pericles* didn't have any furniture whatsoever. *The Merchant of Venice* had two chairs. So that anything that the actors feel or think has immediately got the whole weight of the body behind it.'

It is sometimes said that the high water mark of the RSC's achievements was the 1962 production of *The Wars of the Roses* and that it would have been better to go on working on the basis of the style that it crystallized. Terry Hands disagrees. 'The plays were basically treated naturalistically. Except that John Bury's designs heightened them beyond pure naturalism into a sort of Brechtian approach, but it was still a realist approach – blood and thunder and mud. It was the anti-romantic approach which tied in with the feelings of the early sixties. But essentially it was breaking against a tradition rather than building one, although we kept it on in *Henry IV* and for quite a long time after. *The Revenger's Tragedy* started to take that technique away into a freer world, a more theatrical world. It hasn't been a logical progression, but as theatre got away from its fairy-tale qualities and became something much more meaty and down-to-earth, it seems to have been liberated until in fact it has become more theatrical, more able to do anything it wants. As in Peter Brook's *Midsummer Night's Dream*, which could create its effects by relying on the audience's imagination. *The Wars of the Roses* gave the audience blood and smoke and guns, and there was no costume that didn't look as though someone had ridden twenty miles in it. They came in looking splattered with foam from the horse's mouth, so the audience wasn't being called upon to use its imagination, though it was being re-trained not to expect beautiful costumes.'

Unlike Ronald Eyre, Terry Hands is a firm believer in Ensemble theatre. 'I don't think it's the only way to approach work. All I know is that I'm happier working in that way and working with a group that's been together for some time. Liverpool was a very close group because it was small. We all earned the same amount, suffered the same problems, did everything ourselves. We knew each other's potential. We knew where the dangers lay, we knew what to try and develop in each other and what to take advantage of in each other, and what to guard against in each other. That saved time and it also helped produce some good results.

'In the RSC we also have a policy of keeping together as long as we can. It can produce the same results: that you know the actor well, know where he's strong, where he needs extra encouragement. It enables one to cast a season in such a way that you ask an actor to give you something he can do easily or to give you something that's hard for him, so he stretches, he develops and becomes more of an all-round actor. When you're playing shows in repertory each takes on an extra value from the other. Equally, of course, it has its drawbacks – the actors get bored with each other sometimes, get to dislike each other and it gets a bit claustrophobic. Sometimes you become blinded to things because you're prone to like people so much. But on the whole the drawbacks of the system are outweighed by its virtues.'

For the directors too the fact of working in a group makes a useful difference in four ways. First there is what Terry Hands calls 'the normal interaction of friends. Secondly, we help each other when we get together to cast the season, because in trying to agree to each other's casting the discussion that starts up around the director's view of the play and of whether a particular actor would be good in a particular role can be constructive and helpful.

'Thirdly, there's a system we've used for six or seven years now whereby each director selects one of his colleagues to be a "sounding board" for each production. After you've worked with a designer to produce a model for the set, you show it to the director who's going to be your sounding board. He then asks questions like a devil's advocate, and you explain your intentions. He then comes to your first complete run through and your first club preview. Sometimes to the first dress rehearsal as well – it depends how the play's going. His job then is to say "Six weeks ago you told me you wanted A, B and C. Now I'm seeing C and D. What's happened to A and B?" So at that point, where you can no longer see the wood for the trees, he may be able to tell you where the wood is.' Terry Hands was the sounding board for Trevor Nunn's production of *The Taming of the Shrew* and David Jones's for *The Lower Depths*. Trevor Nunn was sounding board on Terry Hands' *The Merry Wives*, David Jones on his *Merchant of Venice* and both Trevor Nunn and David Jones together on his production of Genet's *The Balcony*.

'The fourth way is that any director is bound to have more contact with some actors than with others. The rapport just happens to be better. So sometimes we're in the position of being able to call in a colleague who has a way of finding the right words to give the right help to a particular actor to explain what it is one's seeking.' But just as the rapport between directors and an actor, being dependent on personalities, varies from time to time, and from person to person, so does the rapport between directors. Each director will find some of his colleagues more helpful than others, and relationships, inevitably, change over the years.

It is sometimes said that the RSC became more democratic when Trevor Nunn took over from Peter Hall, but according to Terry Hands, 'The way in which it has become more democratic really is probably nothing to do with theatre: it's something to do with the country, and to do with the world at this moment – that actually in every walk of life people are wanting to have more to say in where their work goes and what happens to it. In a company like our own the freedom the actors have always had has now become more obvious.' But there are limits beyond which democracy inside a theatre company cannot be taken. To invite actors to participate in discussions on casting would be to open the door to unending argument, and though there are conferences at which general policy is discussed, Terry Hands thinks that changes have to be initiated by the directors. 'It seems to me that whenever there are innovations in theatre, whether administrative or artistic, they are nearly always made by writers and directors. Consequently I know it would be madness – because we've tried it – to have actors anywhere near policy decision. Even when we've asked actors to direct other actors, the style of their directing is fifties, or, if they're older, forties, or, with the very young ones now, sixties, but never seventies. And when you suggest a new way of doing a trial scene or a new way of approaching a play, you nearly always find a resistance, even though it is soon overcome. I think this is part of the very nature of the theatre.

'Writers are the only creative people, as far as I'm concerned, in the theatre. Actors are either good or bad interpreters, directors either good or bad co-ordinators. Actors can use their talent and their ego to express themselves. They can go direct to an audience, stand up in any room and entertain. For a director to express himself or his ego, or his talent he has to operate through other people. The director, therefore, is forced, over a number of years, to develop the arts of persuasion, and patience, and *care* of the actors because it is the only means of getting his way. It is a process of helping someone else to realize something you have in your mind, but it's got to be shared by them or they won't do it. Because they don't *need* to do it. Consequently, as directors, you are looking for the thing that will make the actor more real, or that will present him more advantageously, or will help him in some way. Which means that of necessity you are tending to think of innovations and original approaches by the very nature of your job. This is why I think the initiation of policy should always come from directors.'

One of Terry Hands' earliest productions at the Aldwych – *The Merry Wives of Windsor* – was remarkable for its warmth and its vitality. 'We spent quite a lot of time doing Elizabethan dances – to try and get that sort of élan to it. Otherwise we just worked off the text. But all the time trying not to be clever, but to be loving, I suppose, to like each other. It was the only play he wrote about the middle classes. I think it's one of the finest comedies he ever wrote and a much underrated play. But I think that's because the Folio version of the play makes no sense. It's dated 1623 and by then he'd been dead for eleven or twelve years; the Quartos were often just prompt copies and he seems to have done his plays in different ways on different tours. But altogether there's so much speculation, all you can go on is what works theatrically. And to try and do that play from the Folio is a lost cause. We redid the script to such an extent that we had to print a new version for the understudies. We actually had to type it out and xerox it, because they couldn't follow – I'd made so many changes, juxtapositions, changes of order and Quarto additions and replacements. In fact I wish we'd published the text we used, because judging by the way audiences responded, we'd got closer to the play Shakespeare had intended. I think what actually happened was that they kept changing round, according to the boys they had or the men – I think they probably played it with young men rather than boys. And I think in the Folio all they did was to chuck all the lines together – so that you keep finding in it points where Mistress Page is saying Mistress Ford's line, and Mistress Ford is saying not only her own lines but Mistress Page's. It's not just a question of cutting, it's a question of properly apportioning the different lines which relate to the different characters. There are quite clearly two very different ladies involved, and I think that's part of the problem. But the Quarto of *Merry Wives* is not the very bad Quarto it's usually said to be. I think it was simply a touring version, and therefore much cut, but actually the lines that are in it play better than most of the lines in the Folio. I did a version which was tested daily with actors – and when you get actors as good as Liz Spriggs and Brenda Bruce and Ian Richardson and Brewster Mason, it's really quite a valid litmus paper test. If they can't make a line work, there's something wrong with it. Then you find there's another line in another version and you give them that and that works, and you begin to think well surely that's the one he meant.'

Probably Terry Hands's least satisfactory production – both to audiences and himself – has been Jonson's *Bartholomew Fair*. 'I shouldn't even have attempted it in under ten weeks' rehearsal, because I think it's the most volcanic play I've ever come across. I wanted to do it because I knew it was a tough one. I hadn't quite realized just how rich, how extraordinary, how marvellous. I think it's his finest play and his most comprehensive, in that he uses all the techniques of his other plays in it.

'I believe I was on the right lines. I wouldn't change my approach to the play at all, if I did again. But we opened the play in a rehearsal stage, with a lot of messiness which should have been eradicated. The other major mistake was not to cool down and unify the characters more in terms of costume and behaviour. I left the eccentricities to run wild right from the word go – so there was no progression. I think we made it too sort of Mother Couragey-dowdy, and one could have lifted it more by a very simple change of material in some of the hangings.

'And I think I cut far too much. Perhaps one could start the performance at six, and one should have a break and give them sandwiches or something. But I cut it to the point of mutilation and still was left trying to rush it through in normal theatrical time. I know there are people who hate Jonson and therefore shouldn't come. Those who love Jonson should come for a four or five hour stint. I mean if one doesn't like plays that boil over, don't go to Arrabal, don't go to Jonson, don't go to Triana. I don't think it's a play that's meant to make the audience happy. Surely it's much more of a world picture than *The Merry Wives* – it's not a comedy in the sense that *The Merry Wives* was, about people who would go home at the end of the day to warm drinks and noggins and bowls of milk laced with brandy which you dip your bread into. It is a world of grotesques and ordinary human beings and incredible eccentrics. It's a world of great vulgarity and coarseness – it seemed to me *The Merry Wives* was very much the world of Giles, *Bartholomew Fair* is very much the world of Gerald Scarfe or Ralph Steadman.'

Sometimes he starts on a new production with a clear visual conception, but not always. 'I did feel *Merry Wives* was Elizabethan right from the word go. That was essential, and I saw it entirely in those terms. *Pericles* I couldn't see at all for ages. That developed as we went along. *Bartholomew Fair* one felt was everything and everybody at all times, and somehow one ought to set off on that. But that's a process which is so dangerous that you really need weeks and weeks to try something and throw it away and try something else and throw that away. We had a system where the actors made their own costumes to some extent and discovered them, but we didn't have quite enough time to make that work. I couldn't see *The Merchant of Venice* in visual terms at all, and it took a lot of work with the designer, Timothy O'Brien, before we began to find a world which we started to believe in.'

He begins by thinking about characters as if they were naked. 'This is what this person feels about that person, that's what that person feels about this person – and one thinks of them with nothing on at all. Actually I always think of plays naked first and clothe them as I go along. What clothes do these people wear? Why do they wear them? What is there in the way they behave in the play that would lead them to be wearing these clothes? I spend as long as I can – at least a couple of months if possible – working on the text and just analyzing what it is. Mathematically analyzing it, making charts of the main words that are used. If the word "death" is mentioned fifty times in one scene, subliminally it's going to have an effect on the audience. I thought *Merry Wives* was a play where the predominant imagery was hunting, but in fact when I did all this I found it was absolutely domestic. It was all kinds of things – like sausages and puddings and carpets and bags and the clock and the hour and baskets and laundry and what house one lived in. I think if I'd have read it fifty-five times I still wouldn't have noticed that, because it was something that didn't appeal to me – I don't trust my own opinion of a play at all. When I look at a play, I read one third of what is there, one third of what I would like to be there, and one third I miss altogether. But if you do it mathematically, you memorize the play very well, and you are able to focus on the subliminal effect the play is intended to have on an audience. And then you can decide to back it up, to complement it, or to cut against it.

'With *Pericles* there was nothing domestic at all. All the operative words were to do with gods and stars. It was to do with the imagery of masques, so one needed an approach which was as liberated as that. With *Richard III* it was unquestionably death, death, death, death, heaven, hell, death, disease, animals. The political lines in *Richard III* can be counted on about ten fingers. It's far more to do with the supernatural, and divine orders, and justices. In *The Merchant of Venice* of course it's all financial. After going through that process I approach the designer and say "Okay, we've got a naked actor. These are the word-patterns Shakespeare's using, this is the meaning of the scenes – we think – this is what ought to be going on, so what is he dressed in – if anything?" You start from dressing him practically, so that you don't have a misleading focus in the scene, and then you start to work outwards. What does he need? A stick or a letter or a table or chair – anything in the immediate vicinity of the actor? And when one's done that – where is he?

'Personally I much prefer working in terms of scenery which is *about* the play rather than *of* the play. The actor is *of* the play; it's as well to surround him with what is *about* the play – to enrich what is said. But then the things he actually handles should be – and nearly always are – of the play. A chair or a table is of the play. Whereas the surround – the world he's walking across – is about the play. And in terms of *The Merry Wives of Windsor*, for instance, the floor – that sort of patchwork carpeting, and the patchwork sort of cloth effect at the back – was very much about the play. Warm wool and autumnal colours. Whereas the chairs they sat in, or the goblets or tankards they handled were of the play.

'For *The Merchant of Venice* I used that process. The scenery has nothing to do with Venice – there are no gondolas or chianti bottles or anything of that kind – because I don't think it is about Venice in that sense at all, scenically. It's a play about two people getting married – and as such it can happen anywhere. But obviously Venice and Belmont have to be different, so the scenery is about Venice and about Belmont, as thematic ideas of what they represent to Shakespeare. I'm convinced he didn't ever go to Venice – because of obvious things in the text. If he'd been there, he wouldn't have said them. The clothes they wear are clothes we've invented, contemporary without being modern, rich without being period. They're clothes that can be lived in. It's a play about handkerchiefs and coats rather than cloaks and feathers, whereas the objects they handle are very real, very ordinary, very natural, very naturalistic.'

He also formed very clear ideas about the relationships between the main groups of characters. 'I think there are five pretty clearly defined groups in the play. Antonio, Solario and Salario are all part of one group – merchant venturers, and I think the nearest modern equivalent to that kind of man is a gambler. They're not bankers or involved in anything as safe as that. Antonio is constantly talking about hazarding and dice – about gambling. To be a venturer at that time, you put up money for a boat or you had your own ships and you sent them out. They weren't sausages, they weren't machines, they weren't shares – they had human beings on them. They sailed off and everything was against them – winds, currents, rocks. The play was written in the time of Drake, Raleigh, Frobisher, Hawkins. You might get your boat back loaded with pearls, loaded with gold, silver, tobacco, potatoes, cloths, spice or nothing or scurvy or yellow fever. Lancaster's expedition to the East Indies set off in 1589 and came back in 1593. Three ships came back with four fifths of their complement of men gone, and all the money that had been put into them lost. This play was written around then and probably first performed about 1594 or 1596.

'Antonio has put his entire estate on six or seven ships, and it's a six to one gamble that not one of them gets back. This is a very important point. Because in a way Antonio was competing against investment capital, against Shylock – a man who doesn't gamble, a man who gives a thousand ducats and asks for two thousand back without risking anything. There's no luck or fortune involved, it's "Give it me back by that time with that addition". The first time they meet they argue out the differences between investing (or usury as it's called in the play) and venturing. The major problem of the play is to try to get that across. Because it's something we've not done since the Elizabethan period – not properly. I suppose the nearest modern equivalent to an Antonio is somebody like Onassis with his ships. It's certainly not a Forsyte – Forsytes don't risk money. If you were thinking in terms of the nineteenth century, then I suppose it's somebody like Brunel, who decides to build the *Great Britain*, the first large ship to be made entirely out of iron. That was a sort of gambling. He was a rakish character really, and it was a very dangerous thing to try.

'I think the second major group in the play is the Bassanio, Lorenzo and Gratiano group, who are obviously the spenders, if the first group is the getters. The modern equivalent would be something like the young film stars, the playboys. I think they change, they develop as the play goes on, but they are young aristocrats, people who had money by heredity and have spent it, and they live off people like Antonio. But Bassanio is the other person who could be the Merchant of Venice of the title, because it seems to me he ventures for a lady.

'The play is riddled with gamblers. Portia herself is the prize of a gamble – it's a three-card trick – which one is the queen? Put a pound on it. No, you've lost it. He gambles – he's lost one fortune of his own, one fortune of Antonio's, he borrows three thousand ducats and could lose all that, or gain the whole lot back again or gain a love. Shakespeare parallels the idea of financial venturing and venturing for love – as he does in many of his plays. Romeo looks at Juliet and says "I would venture like a bark upon a stormy sea for such a prize". They talk about bringing back the golden fleece when they've won Portia – when Drake got back from one of his voyages he said he'd got the golden fleece.

'Portia and Nerissa obviously are the prizes. It's like the Wheel of Fortune, you stop it, then you take out an envelope and you hand it to her and say " Have I won?" and she says "Yes, and your prize this week, viewers take note, is me". They're more passive gamblers, but she does finally turn up in the trial scene to gamble her own intelligence and brightness on winning the freedom of the man she loves, Bassanio.

'The fourth group is the Jews, Tubal, Shylock and Jessica. Shylock is not just a Jew, he's a miser and a puritan—" I don't like music. I don't like sounds of laughter. I don't like feasting." The play is about the difference between love's wealth and commercial wealth, the wealth of love where usury is absolutely mandatory – that you should give back more than you're given and that you should demand excess. To balance that against real money and the dangerously real world of money means obviously that Shakespeare has got to work from extremes, and Shylock becomes an extreme. We know that factually the Jews could only be involved in certain functions – old clothes, trade with the East, loan banking. We know that usury was forbidden by the Bible, and yet they had to do it, because that was the only way they could get a living. But Shylock gambles too – he does the longest odds gamble in the play, which is quite uncharacteristic. Which is why the play begins with that type of crisis. He so hates Antonio that he is prepared to gamble three thousand ducats on a pound of flesh, and his odds are something like eighteen to one, because each of the six ships would bring back three times the value of that bond. But it comes off. I think the final group is Launcelot Gobbo and Old Gobbo, who are clearly up from the country. They don't seem to belong in Venice. They are the clowns. But the confusion of Launcelot seems to me to be the touchstone of the play – as so often with the Fools in Shakespeare.

'I think it's a very cosmopolitan play. It's got a Moroccan, it's got a Spaniard, three Jews, it's got Venetians who are obviously Englishmen in a sense, it's got a maid who's a Moor. But Shakespeare is constantly saying "It's not what people are that matters – religion, or colour – it's the way they behave". I mean Shylock says "Hath not a Jew eyes? Prick us, do we not bleed?" Morocco says "Don't dislike me because I'm black, cut me and I've still got the same blood as anybody else." And Portia says very graciously " Look, if I could really choose on my own, you'd stand as fair as any other suitor". It's the way they behave that finally defines them. Morocco's mistake in the choice of casket is not made because he's black but because he's bombastic and wants the wrong things out of life. I think Arragon fails, not because he's a twit but because he's too arrogant, he's too proud. It's what is inside the man that makes him fail. What is inside Shylock, the humanity of the Shylock type of Jew, is Jessica. Now Jessica becomes Lorenzo's wife and is accepted totally into the world. Portia puts her whole house – all that tremendous wealth she obviously has – into the charge of Lorenzo and Jessica. Not just Lorenzo, but Lorenzo *and* Jessica – it's made quite specific. And I think there is a constant justification of what Jessica has done. A constant worry from her of "Have I done the right thing to leave my father?" and a constant reiteration of "The man has ceased to be a man, because he's become so evil, so monstrous, because he wants to kill. He's putting the death of Antonio above everything else". Finally Shylock becomes a murderer.

'The play's got out of balance because there's a great deal of sentimentality now attached to the whole idea of Jewishness and the Jews and Jewish people. If Jessica were a Catholic girl, eloping, and becoming a Protestant or running away from a Catholic dad who told her "You can't have contraception and you'll have ten babies by the time you're thirty-five and all that", we'd say "Thank God she got away from that Victorian, dogmatic, Catholic dad", because we don't happen to be sentimental about the Catholics. But because it's a Jewish dad, it suddenly becomes awful and terrible and "Why is she doing this to that poor old man?" I think Shakespeare supplies enough clues for the redemption of Shylock and Shylock wilfully ignores them. He can't even make up his mind which he likes most, his ducats or his daughter. For the poor girl to have lived in a house where Dad's consistently confusing her with his bags of ducats, seems to me it must have been pretty horrible.'

Terry Hands's production avoided the cuts which are often made into the Jessica sub-plot and avoided special pleading on Shylock's behalf. 'One is very much trying to play the fact that Shylock deserves to forfeit our sympathy. A modern Israeli would surely lose sympathy with Shylock because he would go to the stake rather than become a Christian. But finally when they say to Shylock "You shall also become a Christian", he says "I am content". Come the end he should have said "All right I will try and cut off the pound of flesh", knowing he would kill Antonio and pursue his hatred to the last, and in a strange way he would have died a hero, and it would have been a different play. But he doesn't – he gives in on that, he gives in on everything. And I think what walks out is a man who really deserves to have forfeited our sympathy.'

Preparing for his production of Genet's *The Balcony*, Terry Hands had to do even more textual preparation than on a Shakespeare play. 'There are six versions of the text. Only three thousand copies were printed of the first edition – numbered copies, privately circulated. The play was written in fifteen scenes but in the second edition it has nine and there are nine in the third, but with considerable differences. The fourth, fifth and sixth are largely like the third. Out of all this one had to work back to Genet's original concepts and ideas, which were later distorted because France was in a very shaky state politically when the play was done and he made cuts and changes, taking advice from friends and directors, like Roger Blin, and from Bernard Frechtman, his English translator. He cut out certain Artaud-like ideas, such as bringing on to the stage blood, sperm and tears as personifications. In the version of the play I did with Barbara Wright, we were concerned not simply to translate but to restore his original conception. We did a fifteen scene version and we used every scene he'd written, interpreting it in our own way when it was a purely visual scene without dialogue. We used the ending of the first edition, which was the Lord's Prayer sung, but we incorporated the tomb scene for the Chief of Police, which comes in the second edition but not the first. We tried to put together all the strong and dramatic points from the various editions. Genet uses army jargon in the General's scene and legal jargon in the Judge's scene, so in translating another problem was to find equivalents in English jargon.

'But above all we were concerned to put the play together as a play. When Peter Brook did the play in Paris in 1960 he found the second half almost impossible. According to him it worked in our production because we were using the fifteen scene version, including two revolution scenes. Genet is not a logical writer but his instinct is unerring and he was badly advised in his revisions.'

Having finalized his text, Terry Hands concentrated on producing a clown show. Genet had said that it needed a Grock in every role. Each character was given a clown's white face. 'A clown is a long way distant from what we imagine of a brothel. But I don't think the brothel is what the play is about. It's about politics. For me it's the greatest of the political plays, because it's the only political play not limited by any particular moment in politics. And therefore it's always relevant, and Genet castigates both the revolutionaries and the state. It's a bleak vision but it's a vision of self-seeking and self-obsessions. What he puts down as the roots of almost any political activity is personal obsession, and sometimes he makes it sexual, sometimes it's to cover other weaknesses or failings in personality or in physique. For me this is the truest type of politics. I am bored stiff with productions that put a political slant on Shakespeare's plays because they are only imitations of a fashion. For me politics is the symptom of a disease not the disease itself. Therefore most political plays for me are concerned with symptoms, not with the true disease. Shakespeare's concerned with the true disease, and certainly *The Balcony* is. The politics in it are treated as a symptom; the core of the play is the disease itself – what is going on in human beings. That is not to say that everybody in that play is ill. It's to say that all of them are human.

'One of the great influences behind the play is the funfairs that Genet writes about in his novels – *Our Lady of the Flowers* for instance, where his lover gets caught in the hall of mirrors which are part mirror and part glass. He is screaming with rage, and the veins standing out, because he can't find his way out and people are looking in all around and laughing at him. But they can't hear a thing. Another great influence on the play was the brothel itself. There was, of course, a very famous brothel which he based it upon – the one that Lautrec was in, which had those rooms in it. There are photographs of many of those rooms with those particular amusements carried out. The most popular one was one Genet didn't use, but he talked about it to Peter Brook. You entered your room and you climbed into a railway carriage. A little while later a woman got in wearing a hat and veil and carrying a shopping basket. She sat with her legs together, on the other side of the compartment. Whistles were blown and there were other sound effects as your train apparently moved out, and there was rolling scenery, operated as the old films were, on two spools. During the course of your journey, as your coach shuddered along, you assaulted the lady in the carriage. The brothel is the place where everything is possible, everything is provided, any ideas, any wish, any fulfilment. So it can be the purest desires of people.

'The third influence is the Church and the intensity of Church ritual. Now what do those things add up to? If you look at nineteenth century funfairs they included a theatre and they always had steam organs. People dressed up. Acting, clowning, throwing things and buying things. That's what the play is. Certainly that's how we did it, using those two cores, the church and the circus. Those two things come together in carnival. And it's just like carnival time in Rio de Janeiro. It's political. You attack the state by dressing up as a judge, as a king. Or you dress up as an angel or you carry with you religious emblems. You sing hymns. It's also an orgy: you eat, drink, you debauch. But the two roots of it are in clowning with its satirical dressing up and in religion.'

Madame Irma, then, becomes a female clown, and Brenda Bruce was encouraged to import into her characterization 'a kind of sordid undertow of socks with holes in, and pink nighties with black suspender belts showing underneath.' Barry Stanton, as the Chief of Police, became something like Chaplin as the Great Dictator. 'Surely the man is a clown, his demands, the rhythm of the lines, the explosions of the lines, his effects, which are created always by undercutting or by pratfalls. What is frightening about him is the power he holds. What is comic about him is the man underneath it, the desire for the image. The whole play is a great celebration of the birth of the Chief of Police, the new King. What Genet is saying is "Look inside any peaked cap and you will see the beginning or (if you like) the remnants of a crown". That's where the old autocratic power has gone, and that is the new twentieth-century figure, the Chief of Police. And of course it's a figure that's naïve, like a baby. It's in swaddling clothes, and it seems to me that the plump, pink Barry Stanton amply and totally conveyed this and conveyed it marvellously. I think the only thing that might have made it yet more grotesque was if he'd been older.'

The visual impact of Terry Hands's production was unforgettable. This was one of his most successful collaborations with the designer Farrah. One of their starting points were the two-foot high cothurni Genet asks for. 'These are ordinary little men who put on these great things to be special. Now Irma is described in the first scene, dressed all in black, almost as though she was in mourning. Why? Partly because she presides over the rites of the dead, yes, but also because she wishes to encourage people to dress up in sumptuous clothes and go preening and peacocking in their new robes and putting themselves up another two feet in the air. To make them feel good she would make herself look as black, as small and as unnoticeable as possible. So the cothurni came out of this, they had to be big. In fact we used industrial acid bath cleaning extension feet, which you can walk through vats in.

'The moment one knew that the characters had to be on two foot cothurni one knew that we were in a world where scenery and staging had to be together. We went through fifteen possible sets. We designed a mirror set – layer upon layer upon layer of mirrors. We designed a brothel. Each variation on these prevented the play from taking off into its other areas. There was a sense of claustrophobia and yet there is a sense of great openness. We went on and on until we ended up with the simplest thing of all. If you dress a man up like that, he wants a little cubicle. The thing that really affected us, I suppose, was hospitals – where you draw curtains around a little bunk or form a little cubicle in which somebody may be dying. It came out of a photograph of an Eastern hospital, where there were little curtains all drawn around. It was so like a kind of primitive brothel, too. And then we just used the surround to the stage to suggest the world of mirrors and reflection. We placed the organ above it and the two musicians. I suppose the final impression we were after was a sumptuous funfair with a little hospital room in the middle of it, which constantly changed as one patient after another came into it. But the production had to be able to break out of this and use the whole theatre – Genet always seems to *use* the theatre.'

The experience of directing *Richard III* in French taught Terry Hands a good deal about Shakespeare and about the value of the English language as a weapon in the actor's hand. 'The English actor is famous not so much because of his talent as because of the words that he speaks. His language is free and modern, he can place stresses where he likes, turn or shape a word. We have no gender and no rules. Blank verse can be free or formal. It can swing and spread and go into prose. The freedom the English actor has in pointing the words gives him an advantage over the Continental actor. The French actor has less freedom. Some words are short and have to be spoken short; long words have to be spoken long. Certain repetitions cannot be allowed; others are compulsory. There is the tirade, a long rhetorical speech building to one point. Shakespeare's long speeches are never rhetorical; they can make any number of points. Each word matters, whereas in French each phrase matters. The English actor works on the word, the French actor on the phrase. This gives the French actor more discipline because he's working through the line.

The English actor's strength is his inventiveness. His weakness is his lack of discipline and his laziness, his lethargy. The French actor is not very inventive.

'Doing *Richard III* at Stratford we were aware of the richness of the text but we fell down on the pattern, the tightness, the formal side. In France the transitions between Comedia dell'arte and Greek tragedy, between morality play and Feydeau could be handled in non-naturalistic terms. What I learnt about Shakespeare was how he developed the language. We had gender in Anglo-Saxon and we had rules that governed the order of nouns in Middle English. By Chaucer's time this was going, and he helped the language to get away from the Middle Ages. Wyatt and Surrey started the process of freeing it from strict forms. Marlowe and Shakespeare exploited this. I learnt more about the sharpness and the onomatopoeia in Shakespeare. I saw the way he uses adjectives or adverbs or clusters of them, and how he throws verbs together. I saw what his methods were of achieving the intensification that you very rarely get in prose, communicating through tightly packed sentences.'

One of the features that made the new production of *Richard III* so successful in France seems to have been the pageant element in it. 'One is concerned to please the public at all times – they're the other half of the play – but so often it's more luck than judgment when one strikes the mood of the time. *Richard III* in Paris was the right play in the right place at the right time. I think I've done better productions, but they've been of the wrong play in the wrong place at the wrong time. In 1969 at Stratford the success of the late plays amazed us, but the public seemed to be looking for optimism, for ideals asserted by positive affirmation, for happy endings. In *Pericles* and in *Winter's Tale* you see goodness directly portrayed (instead of being implied by showing wickedness as in *Richard III*) and the public responded tremendously.

'John Barton's *Troilus and Cressida* wasn't well received in Stratford and didn't have a good audience, but when it came to London the public was in a cynical mood and the play slotted into that need. In Paris when we did *Richard III*, what they wanted was grandeur, big theatre, with driving music, torches, banners, melodrama thundering across the stage again. Because they hadn't had that since Jean Vilar in his prime, since

Gérard Philipe. They've had the reduction of plays by Left Wing political slants, reducing them to Brechtian statements. Their classics had become very pretty and their modern work very extreme, and suddenly, judging by the reviews and the reactions, everybody wanted big theatre, at a time when, in England, we're heartily sick of it and looking for something lighter, more optimistic, more joyful.'

Turning to T. S. Eliot's *Murder in the Cathedral* and directing RSC actors in it, Terry Hands was aware of the dangers of approaching it in the same way as Shakespeare. 'Eliot isn't concerned with working through a verse form that can be used and then broken off for the sake of variation; he's concerned with using poetry as an everyday spoken language. He uses the *caesura*, the breath in the middle of the line. He works off alliteration for his attacking points. It's preciser and more consistent than Shakespeare, but where he becomes very exciting and Shakespearean is in his use of onomatopoeic words. "Your sin soars sunwards." His use of Anglo-Saxon alliterative forms is fascinating. "Power is present". "A temple tomb monument of marble".

'Of course it's not a play in any accepted sense. It's simply concerned with death and martyrdom, and it is itself a long ceremonial, a long prayer. The language and the content, which are precise, demand a similar precision of staging. It is God's pattern that's being discussed: the actor's pattern becomes important to it. The play itself provides a fascinating exercise in poetry reading and in choreography, yet it must come over as neither. It's couched in a form intended to be as close as possible to that of *Everyman*, where in order to explain things you separate them. In a morality play, if a man has a decision to make between one course of action and another, you personify both choices and all three then debate what to do. You have a good angel, a bad angel and a man in the middle. By the time you come to Shakespeare the angels are abandoned and put into the one man, who then conducts a debate with himself, like Launcelot Gobbo, between his conscience and his devil. Eliot goes back to the old form, so the debating aspect is very strong.

'But the content is starkly contemporary. It was written in

the thirties, the time of the depression, the last fling of imperialism, the last attempt at assertion. That awful anonymity and that apparent sense of aimlessness that you see in thirties newsreels are the opposite of the wonderful individualism you see in Shakespeare's characters. The people we see in Eliot are the colour of the earth they work on. No one throws out his chest. He looked at the sea of bowler hats crossing Westminster Bridge, the acres of rubbish flowing down the Thames. That's the sterile world he starts from, the "living and partly living".

'In that world all that could come was the hard assertive statement. The thirties were the cradle of Fascism in Germany, Spain and Italy, while in England more people were Moseleyites than would be admitted today. In *Murder in the Cathedral* you find the Knights are very much like the Fascist order, and that Eliot, a passionate Christian, is making the assertive statements of Catholic dogma in an almost Fascist sense. He ties the sense of barrenness to the old Priest-King legend. They are waiting for the blood of a saint to fertilize the spirit, as the winter land will be fertilized by the coming of spring. The production of the four Knights that Eliot himself liked best was in a French production in 1945, where he said they knew exactly what it was like to live under a Fascist dictatorship, so they took the Knights seriously.

'Perhaps the feeling of aimlessness today is similar. If the theatre is a mirror of what people want it must be significant that it's thrown up two assertive statements like *Godspell* and *Jesus Christ Superstar*. The mystic figure is real. Christ is on the stage and he's a lunatic. He dogmatizes, refuses to be argued out of things. Like a Buddhist monk burning himself, he lets himself be killed. Both shows seem to respond to a desire for mysticism, because the church is rapidly demystifying itself – which I think is a mistake – and it goes with the special cults which are springing up but which will probably never catch on because to do that they'd need martyrs and the government today is far too clever to allow martyrdom.

'The martyr is rather like an atomic bomb. You need to let it off to prove it will go off but the moment you've destroyed it you need another. So you maintain a sense of power and a sense of sickness in the air. You need another martyr to prove that there can be such things as martyrs, to give an impression of the strength of the ideal for which they're prepared to die. So far as the Christian church is concerned, the fall-out from the martyr is wholly good. But Eliot is careful to link his church, his religion and his spiritual life to Nature, and to that extent too it's contemporary with our concern about pollution. We need our Johnny Appleseed as well as our St John.

'For me the three great classics of the twentieth century are *Waiting for Godot*, which is based on the idea of clown, *The Balcony*, which is based on carnival – which is clowns and church together – and *Murder in the Cathedral*, which is based on the church. No-one could be more different than the Irish Beckett, the French Genet and the Anglo-American Eliot, but they were all born and brought up at about the same time and the three plays are remarkably akin.'

For Terry Hands the ideal actor is half way between a monk and a madman. 'The profession requires peculiar qualities. An actor in our company will get one evening off a week and he'll get his Sundays, though not all of them. He gets two weeks holiday a year, normally at Christmas, when it's almost impossible to find the sun. He has to be prepared to work thirteen hours a day and his private life has to be lived between eleven o'clock at night and ten o'clock the following morning. This makes for a kind of monkish existence, dedicated to a particular discipline, which should include mental and physical preparation for his work, which is to be constantly prepared to interpret and communicate whatever text is given to him. He needs to keep himself healthy and he needs a knowledge of his own weaknesses. Because of the way theatre is developing he needs to prepare himself for singing and dancing, as well as for the centre of his craft. The majority of actors come only a minimum of the way towards fulfilling those criteria, but even a minimum forces their lives towards a kind of monasticism.

'On the other hand an actor must be sufficiently free, inventive, emotionally and neurotically alive – nerve-endings tingling, emotions churning over – to be fairly mad, and responsive to anything that might happen in a performance after the preparation has been done, when he's playing in front of a thousand people. It's not only the new impetus from the actors he's playing with, it's the impetus from the audience. His training, his monasticism are only needed in order to make those skills into a second nature, so that his instincts can be released to respond to whatever stimuli are pushed upon him. So he has to be slightly mad. His explosiveness, his irresponsibility are usually a good sign.

'It is paradoxical that it has to exist side by side with his monasticism, and most actors I've known find that paradox very hard to live with. The strains it sets up manifest themselves in different ways – eccentricities, curious personal habits, breakdowns. It's a difficult life, and the English actor tends to make it infinitely more difficult by pretending on top of all that that he can live a normal life. This becomes an excuse for laziness and a lack of preparedness. He doesn't fulfil fully the criteria of either monk or madman, and yet he suffers in his life the drawbacks of both. Those actors who seem to me to cope best with their careers and to serve the public best, recognize that that is what their life is, and organize things accordingly. I think time is wasted in rehearsal through a non-recognition of this, and it's also a failure to recognize this that leads to a theatre which verges on therapy and to that kind of safely reduced level of performance which we've come to recognize as the norm. To me the most exciting actors to watch and to work with have been those who have most completely been midway between the monk and the madman.'

RONALD EYRE

⋘∘⋙

'You see I don't really want to direct non-stop. I would prefer
to direct one show a year, and spend the rest of the time
writing, doing book programmes on the radio, and interviewing Marie Rambert on the television or whatever. I fear
very much the feeling of being – on my passport – a *director*,
because I think that that puts one into a sort of profession –
and I don't wish to join. I find for instance I suffer frequently
from book starvation. It's an almost physical thing: I know I
haven't touched anything other than me and my concerns
for a long time. If you've got to do a book programme on the
radio this is a marvellous occasion for reading six books in a
week, doing a broadcast, and suddenly you've read a novel
which you were not very interested in for a start but just the
very fact of its being absolutely outside your usual orbit is
enriching. I'm sure that if I were a full-time theatre director,
I would be out of it in about a year. It sounds very amateurish,
but there are very few professional skills that seem to me to be
absolutely essential to a director. But the thing that seems to me
absolutely essential is a sort of richness, repose in a large area
from which you suck life.'

These are unusual sentiments for a director, but as an under-
graduate at Oxford (where he was a contemporary of John
Schlesinger) Eyre had been more religious than theatrical. He
went on to become a schoolmaster and after four years applied
for a job in BBC Television which he saw advertised in *The
Times*. Like many of the best people who apply for BBC
jobs, he was turned down, but he was lucky. 'The head of that
department had a campaign on against the Appointments
Department, she, a woman, claiming that they always rejected
the best candidiates. Therefore she went through the rejected
lot – and I was one of them – and she got me out. So when
I went to the Board, I was aware that one person was vividly

on my side and determined that I should get the job.'

He has written over twelve television plays, and most of them he directed himself, but at the end of the sixties he was still almost unknown in the theatre. He had never directed in London except at Stratford East and the Hampstead Theatre Club. And in January 1970 he had still done only about eight productions in the theatre. But then he directed Donald Howarth's *Three Months Gone* at the Royal Court with Jill Bennett and Diana Dors. After that he was suddenly in enormous demand, and since then he has orbited through the West End and all three of our big subsidized theatres – the RSC, the National and the Royal Court. He directed Boucicault's *London Assurance* for the RSC at the Aldwych, *Mrs Warren's Profession* at the National, *Much Ado about Nothing* for the RSC at Stratford, John Mortimer's *A Voyage Round My Father* in the West End with Alec Guinness, and Charles Wood's *Veterans* at the Royal Court with John Gielgud.

He explains his early life by saying 'I didn't really wake up till I was about thirty. I don't like fitting into systems and going to school and university I found myself in a series of systems, with which I'd got to cope. This produced rashes of one sort or another – actual physical rashes. I had a deep resentment at being pigeonholed. I think it was only when I came to my senses that I realized that in fact theatrically this was probably one's most valuable asset – to refuse to join the club, whatever it happened to be, and to go in always having to start from scratch.'

He would never anchor himself to working permanently with the same company – quite early on he turned down a chance of taking over Birmingham Rep. For him each production is a matter of starting on 'a new work, with new people. And you try to make yourself new.' And he is unfashionably unconvinced of the virtues of ensemble theatre. *London Assurance* had already been cast when he agreed to direct it. 'This relieved me of certain sorts of decisions and agonies. I just had to work with what was there. And the effect of their having worked together as an "ensemble" – I didn't really find it to be different from any other company. They just seemed to be a well cast company, a cast from out of the blue. Recent trends have been to believe that people work better if they've worked together before. I think people can limit, hate, even maim each other when they've been together a long time. Except when they are well cast or when they are convinced of what they are doing, where they are going and with whom.

'I have never been able to understand theatre directors and theatre boards who announce an *intention* of having an "ensemble". It's as if Saul of Tarsus were to announce his *intention* of seeing a blinding light on the road to Damascus. "Ensemble" – the word – makes sense to me when used to describe the rare concurrence of great talent and energy and love and practice in an event for which no-one can allocate individual credit but neither can anyone be removed without loss. "Ensemble" is a blessing – I'm sounding a bit theological as if it were some sort of grace – and is as likely to happen among a cast assembled piecemeal for one play as among a company that's lived, loved and hated together for years. If not, how has it come about that in recent years the most lauded "ensemble" playing has been at the Royal Court where, whatever the ambitions of its artistic committee, plays are picked, cast and directed piecemeal from scratch? When people began thinking that generosity from one actor to another within a production was a good thing, and that an actor should be prepared not just to play the big part, but to play other parts – which leads to the sort of group you get at the National Theatre or the RSC . . . the point at which that thinking happened was when the theatre was mostly a matter of the most blind and uninformed type-casting by a commercial management. Now that the history of the RSC and the National has broken that, one can look at the advantage of the former system, which is a possibility of accurate casting, which in this new company theatre may not be very easy. The bad side of the permanent company is that you get second best casting with very very good actors. You're not dead down the centre of the part, which is something different from crude type-casting. In a part of a certain kind there is a chemical movement which must be paralleled by something in the actor playing it and that is the quality you're casting for.'

He remembers with pleasure some of the pre-RSC acting at Stratford-on-Avon like Keith Michell's performance as Achilles and Leo McKern's as Ulysses in an earlier production of *Troilus and Cressida*. 'I suppose it would in many people's minds pale beside the RSC's recent *Troilus* but there's no doubt in my mind that there was a sort of vigour about the earlier casting which certainly wasn't in the later one. Maybe it's the ascendancy of the director in company theatres which has made the impact of individual performances feebler. You had a curious kind of fit-up feeling in the earlier RSC productions. And the actors were fighting for survival in a way which may be appropriate to the plays. I don't see there is any point in fighting against the English tradition, which does exist – doesn't it? There are large parts and small parts. A certain belligerence and prickliness is not always counter-productive in the theatre. Take *Mrs Warren*. The actors, half of them intruders on the National Company, carved up their ground, stood on it and competed with each other. In a strange way they were serving the play. It's called "enlightened self-interest".'

His approach to a new company and a new production could hardly be more unlike Peter Brook's: the idea of starting with mirror exercises is anathema to him. 'For me at least the way not to relax and grow would be to sit and scrutinize your neighbour. Really I'd have to find a common object and look at it – it doesn't matter what it is – but if everyone looks at each other, I'd be likely to freeze. Whereas if you turn away and look at an object or work on a thing, then it's co-operative, you're alongside each other looking at something outside yourself. Therefore I would always need to start working on something other than "us" – a third element. It doesn't matter if it's an achieved text or some exercises or digging a trench, but you need something outside yourself to work at. An actor seems to me only to be able to work when he's presented with obstacles – just as if you put a piece of paper over a penny and rub it with a pencil the pattern's going to be what's underneath, it's got nothing to do with the paper working on itself. And one wants the friction between that person and an obstacle, and it's my job as a director to get the actor to locate the obstacles in a situation or a text. Sometimes even to *create* obstacles – to get the actor's imagination working.'

Mrs Warren's Profession has only six characters but three of Ronald Eyre's cast were new to the National Theatre. Coral Browne, who played Mrs Warren, had already been approached before Ronald Eyre was. 'Sarah Badel (Vivie) was an import from outside and that was just because I think that part is extremely difficult to play and needs someone with the equipment that she's got. Bill Fraser came from outside because the company could not easily provide a Sir George Crofts. My insistence on outside recruitment was a challenge to the whole company idea. At Stratford, say, you know there's going to be a line of parts, Isabella, Ophelia and so on, and there's going to be a line of fellows – bloodsome fellows – Iago and Macbeth and whatever. So the same people are going to play them and in a curious way there's a stability about that sort of casting. I think that RSC is more blessed than the National in that at least they've got a fellow who wrote twenty odd plays, at the centre of their work – Shakespeare defines it and also defines the way the company is recruited. The problem with the National Theatre, I think, is that if you do *Cyrano* and *Hedda Gabler*, and you do *Mrs Warren's Profession* and then maybe a Shakespeare and *Philoctetes* and *A Flea in Her Ear*, there is no known company which can possibly cope with that width of material. So in a curious way one's driven to doing what has happened with *Mrs Warren's Profession*, which is really a recruitment from outside of people you've thought proper for that particular play.

'The first thing we did was to observe every stage direction absolutely literally. If Shaw says you sit down, you sit down, and the disposition of furniture is precisely what he asks for. There is one deviation from Shaw's staging, which is something to fit the National Theatre stage, and that causes untold trouble, that one deviation, and we have sometimes to imagine what it would be like if we had observed exactly Shaw's staging. Because there's a geometry in his stage directions, which is not just French's acting edition – a report after the fact. It's part of the creation of the play as it goes on, and if you're going to respect the words and say them, I see no reason why you can't respect the stage directions and do those. Up to the last two weeks of the rehearsal period we leaned on Shaw's staging, put pressure on it and explored the stage geometry as well as the words. Then we felt free to deal with whatever the strengths and weaknesses or wishes of certain actors may be. And then we could start turning it around a bit.

'Of course the way in which Shaw writes demands a lot of confidence in an actor. *Mrs Warren* is a highly emotional play, highly charged. The characters go headlong at each other but they explain themselves at such lengths, with such elaboration, that it's almost like turning a person inside-out, a stage anatomization. The inner process which in some other play might come out in one expletive in the text is elaborately verbalized live. But what you cannot do is to put the passion of the one expletive into the whole speech. You have to find some cool way of serving it up.'

One of the reasons the play appeals so much to Ronald Eyre is that none of the places in which the action is set belongs to the characters. 'The outside and inside of the cottage in Sussex hired for the summer, the outside of a vicarage leased in an odd way from a Bishop. And premises in Chancery Lane and the feeling of dead ground, of no man's land; and these great confrontations go on in this territory, so that possession, familiarity and all that is not allowed. You fight on alien ground. It has something to do with the curiously dead relationship between the characters – the only nexus between them is a cash one. They're economically tied together and the source of their food is the only thing really they have in common. In all other ways they breathe an alien air. That character Praed who comes on and talks about art, for instance, talks to this girl who read maths at Cambridge – they're using the same language and appearing to sit alongside each other in a garden but in fact they could be on different planets. So with Mrs Warren and Vivie. Mother and daughter, maybe, but they have the air of orphans. That is what I believe the play is about. A desolation alongside which Pinter looks cosy. In Shaw's own output I just don't know any other piece quite like that play except *Widowers' Houses*. They are the plays that make me tingle.'

For actors like Ronald Pickup (Frank) who had worked with Peter Brook it may have been surprising that Ronald Eyre wanted to start by meticulously following stage directions which were nearly seventy years old, but after about seven weeks of rehearsal none of them had been changed. The blocking had been done very rapidly: the significance of what they were blocking was discovered much more gradually. 'Certain chunks of scenes which we've done according to Shaw are still done according to him – but – by sticking to what he suggests and somehow getting a feel of what it's about, a different element comes into a scene. An answer to the question "Who's controlling it?" All right, a character is sitting or standing – it doesn't matter – but who's in charge? What's at stake? That matters. And the clue to the answer lies in the stage directions.

'The beginning of the second act, for instance, is quite magnificent. Three of the adults – that is Mrs Warren, George Crofts and the Parson – come and sit around, and they're extremely bored with life in the country. At first in rehearsal we were doing it without knowing who in fact was the mover in that scene. It was a sequence of lines almost, but we respected Shaw's placing. Then we realized that if Frank, the boy, is in a pivotal position at the back of the table, for instance, sitting, looking at these three older people, he becomes a sort of puppet master. They are further downstage than he is, so they can't observe him but he can observe them. And then all of a sudden you realize that the whole structure of the lines is a form of *tease*, and that the weariness, the feetache, the desire not to be in the country, which is going on under the embarrassment of discovering old flames and so on is something which is being played upon by the fellow behind. Now if, say, I'd been directing that without the benefit of knowing where he wanted to place the people, I don't know where I would have put Frank – he could be moving somewhere – but I'm sure it would have taken quite a lot of work and wit to discover something which Shaw in fact provides the material for. Of course it doesn't ignite immediately. But when it did ignite Ronald Pickup ran the scene. He created the pauses and the malice. It's terribly cool. Which is the attitude of the young generation in this play.'

Other plays, of course, have to be approached quite differently. With John McGrath's *Events While Guarding the Bofors Gun* Ronald Eyre went into rehearsal without any clear idea of movements or positions or stage action. 'What I think I started with was a very firm idea of the time of day, the state of the weather, the length of time those men had been at that job and the pressures on them. So what I did was to define them in their action, not by plotting whether they were left or right, but deciding precisely what pressures they were under at the time. If a temperature is below zero, as it was in that play, it's extremely important to keep shutting the door. You can't keep it open for a second. That results in a whole series of physical pictures of coming through with your balls freezing off, and so on. As a director one could think of it being plot moves but the more sensible way to the right complexity is to put the actor – or help the actor to get – into a pincer which is going to force him willingly, happily, to keep what he does within certain limits. Cold will result in his moving a certain way, his body will go differently, the way he wears his clothes will be different, his hands will hang differently, and so on. He'll not handle guns so well, and if there's a fire he'll tend to get near it. So you don't think about the flower arrangement of actors on bunks, you think that who's strongest gets to the fire for longest. As the rehearsals went on I knew I could say "Well anybody in the audience is free to say that they don't like it but they wouldn't be free to say that it doesn't exist and exist strongly".

But how do you go about involving actors in the kind of physical pincer that you're creating for them? You've got to make this real – the cold and so on. Do you say directly to them 'You are feeling cold' or do you create a kind of mood in which that cold figures?

It's a sort of nursery school teaching in one sense. You just must simply create an atmosphere in which everybody's allowed to make mistakes and think their own thoughts and throw in things. On the question of exploring, say, cold – it varies so much from actor to actor. If an actor is unimaginative, I see no reason why one shouldn't say "It is extremely cold, you know, and that would lead to this and this, wouldn't it?" With somebody else, all of a sudden they'll give a shudder and they've got it solo. You work with the material you've got, but I think to try and impose something on them will always seem self-defensive and curiously self-laudatory. I certainly don't want anybody to go on stage looking like my creature.'

If Ronald Eyre has to check himself during rehearsals it's not so much from imposing on actors as from acting things out in front of them. During rehearsals of *A Voyage Round*

My Father Alec Guinness said of him 'He's an extremely good actor but of course we can't spare him to be one because he's too useful as a director.' Eyre says himself 'I think that I'm really an actor, I mean if everybody's got an appropriate label, then that's what I am. So I swing extremely rapidly into wild improvisation of what somebody in a play might be doing. I have to check this, because it doesn't respect the rate at which some actors work and it can be daunting. And irresponsible. I've found that's something I have to repress. But one does fool about. It's prerequisite number one, almost, in rehearsal, to prove that the director can be as big a mess as anybody else. I had a meal with an actor the other night and it started off by his being extremely complimentary about a particular director. After two glasses of Chablis there followed a stream of vitriol of an unspeakable kind about the same director. If you can't stand being handled by fools, if you don't think you have that in you which can resist the interference of people who may know less than you do, you obviously can't afford to be an actor. I think most actors are terribly good at keeping afloat. They have a sort of buoyancy – they'll get on and won't fall down and so on. But if you create an atmosphere in which a sort of risky honesty can happen, you'll find you'll uncover vast hopes and miseries. And the more they can come out and be dealt with properly within the company – I don't mean I have a diagnosis and a remedy, I mean the more we recognize that they exist – the greater the respect from one actor to another and the greater the illumination of the play and so on.'

The plays Ronald Eyre has directed have little, if anything, in common with each other. 'Unlike *Mrs Warren's Profession* and unlike *Bofors Gun, London Assurance* is about kindness, sweetness, embracing and loving, it's about good feeling, generosity. I think I was principally attracted by the fact that there were so many things about it which I considered to be unrevivable. I liked the fact that there was nothing remotely modish, nothing up-to-date. Even in its own terms it's a backward-looking play, the end of a line – enfeebled. It's a boulevard play, it's the highest form of boulevard play. And you suddenly see that lurking underneath it is a powerful statement. Sir Harcourt Courtly for instance, is the person who has a relationship with his mirror. And there are three other

relationships between men and women in the play. They are of
quite different kinds – one more commercial, one absolutely
romantic, one curious – that of Lady Gay Spanker and Mr
Spanker. And these are an affront to this man who is doomed
by the fact that he's just got his mirror and himself. That's
what appeals about the play: its secret riches lurking underneath what looks jaded and old. The first line – the character
called Cool says "Half past nine and Mr Charles not yet
returned! I'm in a fever of dread." – Well if as a playwright
you've got the sort of cheek to do that, I tend to say "I am
in the presence of a friend". It's a pastoral, in a strange way.
I like the vision: it was the dance of the blessed spirits really.
They are privileged people, they are wholesome, they're free.
They live in a flowery place. It's separated off, a bower of
bliss, an alien world, the golden world. Anyway it's an absolutely ideal picture of what one hoped might have been, or
might to some people be or to me one day be a possibility –
of the ease and real niceness. Not a negligible quality. I mean
a palpable, great big strong quality, strong niceness. Because
that's what I think the appeal of the play is.

'When I first read the script I fell for the play not as a
thing achieved on the page but as something that – with about
a fifth rewritten – could work. Although I did write characters in, and wrote whole scenes in the play, I never at all felt
that I was pilfering and twisting. It was like being in the
presence of somebody of rather prodigal talent a bit pissed. He
wasn't getting to the end of his sentences so I said "Well,
look you've forgotten about this character". For instance, the
maid, Pert, only has one scene in the original, which starts
off with a long soliloquy so it looks as though she's going to
be developed a bit. But she never appears again. Boucicault
just forgot about that scene. The lawyer disappears long before
the end. I felt I was just dealing with somebody who didn't
have the impulse to bring his play to conclusions and what I
was doing was a sort of fulfilling job. If my interference
worked, that was what made it work. And it's such a *used*
texture of a play and follows such an ancient frame, that of
eighteenth-century sentimental comedy. So the guide-lines are
there – put down not by Boucicault but by English drama,
in a way. So you know the tradition he's working in, and even
if he cares not to fill out his characters, or loses those pages, or

never gets as far as you'd like him to, you know roughly what he's working for.'

Had Boucicault been alive one feels Ronald Eyre and he might have collaborated, and in *Three Months Gone* the work with Donald Howarth was very much a collaboration. 'He came to all the rehearsals and it was really a co-production – that is, he would fiddle things and I would fiddle things and we would work together. It's a most private play, in a way, and then of course you do it in the open. The fact that it is laughable at and seeable by a lot of people is to me quite miraculous, when the writing itself is really quite arcane and something very much to do with Donald Howarth in private. I went and stayed with him in Wales, and I decided I couldn't direct it, because I couldn't make head or tail of quite a lot of it. I told him this and then he said "Well I'm Alvin and I'm Mrs Hanker. And I am Anna." We went through all of this and then I realized none of the normal guide-lines would help and I began to look for others.

There was a production in Holland afterwards in which the director chose to assert his presence by having the light changed whenever he decided that Howarth's characters went into a fantasy, and I believe at some point he even went into slow motion. Of course that is a real misreading of the play, because the whole point of it is about a co-existence of a real-life and the life of fantasy, even a challenge to the audience to say which is which. Time is disrupted and there is an arbitrariness of time and event, as if the author were saying "And what's more, I can do what I like with my characters." And he does. Time after time he rats on the securities he's given his audience. I'm not sure that that's altogether wise but he does it, and he's very successful. It was a very thrilling thing to do and obviously the natural enmity – I don't mean this in any personal sense – of those two ladies, Jill Bennett and Diana Dors, and the two fellows, Alan Lake and Richard O'Callaghan, tugged the play in all directions. You wouldn't have got that cast from the pot-luck of a permanent company.'

Ronald Eyre is now offered many more scripts than he accepts and his main criterion is always the quality of the writing. When he was approached to direct Edna O'Brien's *A Pagan*

Place at the Royal Court, his intention was to say no. 'I went away one week-end. I said I'll read it once more, and pause a bit in order to show respect. Then say no. But it was terribly good. Undeniable stuff. So I said yes.'

One of the best and most carefully written scripts he has directed is Charles Wood's play *Veterans*. 'He types it like free verse on the page, guiding the director in matters of stressing and shaping. He does it too, I think, in order to indicate that rapid rewrites or paraphrases which are nearly right aren't right enough. I know nobody like him: his words are really *pebbled* and its absolutely what he has chosen to say, what he wishes. He seems to have to mint the inflection as well as the sense of the language. He rewrites extremely readily if he has to, and he also rewrites extremely fast, but he wouldn't like lines invented by actors or directors to be written in.

'One oddity of the piece is that the man who says all the words – the part played by Gielgud – is in a way not the leading part. And that was a problem. When you read it you do get a slightly out-of-focus feeling from the text because you think a great deal of care and love and observation is being lavished on somebody whose predicament doesn't exist, because he's entirely complacent. Whereas there is another man alongside him very much aware of what he is as an actor and where he's going and how far he's fallen, a sort of Lucifer character, who is comparatively unexplored. Now let's say Charles Wood were to be writing that play without having had the experience of working on the film *The Charge of the Light Brigade*, and therefore getting to know John Gielgud, I think possibly his balance would have shifted rather more in favour of Dotty, the character John Mills plays, and away from the Gielgud character.'

It is also very difficult to direct an actor playing a character based on himself. 'Are other things about the person in life relevant as background to the character in the play? With what authority – and with what limits of authority – does an actor play himself? If that actor – not that he did – said "During this scene I should be slowly changing into my bathing costume, because that's what I do on these occasions" should one then say "Well of course, since it's you, then you must"? This was a problem for him too. In the case of the other character, the one that John Mills played, it is known he's a spoilt film-star (not John Mills but that character) and he is known to have had a rocky married life and to "flash" it frequently. With what freedom do you say to anybody playing that part "Well we're actually going to use a lot of you in this"? I think that's one of the difficulties. We all felt it.'

Partly for these reasons it took a very long time to shape the production. 'One had a lot of good ideas which Charles Wood approved and all the cast approved and you did it and that was fine – for that day. Then, curiously enough, it absorbed itself: the play went dry again and you had to have another notion. The feeding in of notions was extraordinary in that piece. So we never felt we were coasting. And we certainly never felt we were arriving. By the time we opened the pre-Royal Court tour in Edinburgh, there was a shape there but a vast amount of rehearsal had to go on on the road. And it wasn't something I didn't expect to happen. I knew that that would be the process. We very much learned as we went along.'

The problems presented by John Mortimer's *A Voyage Round My Father* were very different. This was a less precisely calculated piece of writing, less anguished, more open-ended. 'It's very urbane, and, in a marvellous way, carefree. That's what quite appealed to me. It was like a scattered talker. You couldn't deny that he was shaping the sentences very well, nor could you deny that if you'd set him a different set of obstacles he would have got over them equally elegantly. Built into the script was an admission of its limitations. It was deliberately unpretentious. I mean it was about a particular man and a particular house and so on, and it didn't claim to ring any bells beyond that. If they were rung – as obviously they must have been for the play to have the sort of success it had – it didn't aim at ringing them.

'John Mortimer was not really *plunging into* fiction. He wasn't really making a *character* at all. He was drawing on a very recent memory of his father for certain idiosyncrasies and so on. But what do you mean by "idiosyncrasies" when the man who has them is a powerful and wayward tyrant and the scribe who writes them is his emergent son? I think this play is rather like "Notes towards a play about my father". If he looked at it in twenty years from now, Mortimer may say "That bit is trivial" or "There's much more to be said about him" or "There is an angle on this man which will unify everything I've got to say about him" – instead of depending on separate episodes to carry themselves.

'For the whole cast it was extremely difficult to act, because you have to come on in mid-stream, in mid-action, and you mustn't look as though you're working off bogus energy like people at the end of a pier. On the other hand you've got to come on without the situation you're in having been prepared for, and knowing that it's never probably going to be resolved. There will be a sort of tag line, say, at the end of a scene which is equivalent to "That's all for now folks". And the resolution of all is "The man dies". Unlike most plays this one provides no convenient handrails for staggering actors.'

Ronald Eyre found that his interest in the problems the script set him was more technical than usual. 'I looked at this piece which had been written first of all, I think, as a series of radio sketches, and then as a television play. I wanted to find some sort of stage equation, which could cope with the changing vista. Our solution – Alec Guinness's, Voytek's and mine – was this sort of stark garden using a few pieces of furniture – a ladder, a table, a chair – to do all the jobs. It was an exercise in stage ingenuity – as near as I'll get to chess.

'And this staging gave the context that Alec Guinness needed to start and work. If it had been more fussy, more mechanical or if there had been more mobility about it – if something had slid on bearing a table or a chair or a bit of a law court – it would have challenged the remarkable thing he was attempting to do. I think Guinness's acting is related to classic Japanese acting in the sense that he likes whatever appears – an angel or a snow storm – to be in known terms, not to depend on surprise mechanism. There is a pathway to walk on, and a stage to perambulate and a language with which to cope with whatever it is you're doing – and an exit place. And that's what he'd got on the Haymarket stage. If Trevor Howard had been acting the part, who knows how the way of mounting it might have changed? Or if Michael Redgrave, who took over from Alec Guinness, had been playing from the beginning.'

Ronald Eyre is a thorough-going empiricist. No one could accuse him of imposing a style making a play or a group of actors into a vehicle for his own personality. 'I hate the gauleiter director who directs people like traffic. I haven't got the gall to put people into impossible strenuous positions. I can't do what Eisenstein did to whoever played Ivan the Terrible. That almost dislocation-of-the-neck acting. But then again, I suppose, if on any particular play I had a vision as powerful as Eisenstein's in the cinema, there's no saying what I'd do.' Yet even where he does a lot of rewriting, as in *London Assurance*, it is not in order to adapt the script to any preconceived ideas, and if *Three Months Gone*, *Events While Guarding the Bofors Gun* and *Veterans* could easily be mistaken for work by three different directors, this is because the plays themselves pointed in three different directions, and he followed. 'One of the difficulties is that I see the opposite side of any situation. No sooner has a sentence left my mouth than I've got the opposite sentence pretty well framed and ready to follow it out. It's the same with staging. You have to have an idea before you can start – yet an idea becomes a straitjacket as soon as you've had it. There's got to be room for many things to move about in a play. If I put my personal stamp on it crudely and assertively, what that means is that I limit the reverberations to the ones that I wish to happen, and my intention is that the source of the limitations should be seen to be me. Of course any director does limit the reverberations, but I prefer to think that the limitation is in the situation, which it's my job to make precise for the actors. I would hope you could never see a show of mine and say that the shape or the discipline had been imposed by me. Because the process of rehearsal and staging has been to confront people with a situation in which they have decided their own limitations for themselves.'

If he has developed as a director, it is hard to describe the form that development has taken except by saying that he has achieved a greater flexibility. As he sees it himself, he has begun to regain some of the qualities he had as a child and lost as an adolescent. 'As a child I liked painting and fiddling with objects. Then I stopped handling things and wrote about handling them instead – i.e. I had a literary schooling. And there's no point in denying, just to be in the fashion, that I seem *so far* to need a text before work can begin. That's where I feel secure – if I have the playwright's thoughts by proxy. All the same I don't *direct* by proxy (you know what I mean – paper clips on a ground-plan at night, actors on a stage-cloth in the morning). More and more I need and like the risk and absorption of knowing everything about a play *except* exactly what's going to happen next in rehearsal. This is a sort of confronting of things and the surprises of things that went underground when I was a child and are coming out again. Not before time either.'

No doubt he is also right to feel that he has become more relaxed in rehearsals. 'I think I talk less. I obviously want to avoid the impression of sitting back and never giving anything but I think I am sitting back more and giving less of what I'm thinking. I ask more questions. I need decreasingly at the end of the day to count my small change and say "We have achieved X, Y and Z". What I'm doing is being alongside people who are working at their own rates, and if the thing has life in it it's going to happen without my reliving everything and appearing to spin it out of my middle.' Like most directors he sometimes has to apply the brakes to his own intelligence because an actor's rate of working may be slower. 'I get quite rapid images from reading a play, notions of how you might do it. I would like people to be much freer about trying three things at once instead of doing half a thing and then looking round for approval before they inflate it even into one thing.'

Some directors take little interest in a production once it is successfully mounted; Eyre keeps going back. 'But I don't at all sit back and enjoy it as an audience would. What they are watching is the results of pressures. I'm interested in the pressures themselves and whether they are being kept up. Any scene is triggered off in a certain way by the writing, then by us in rehearsal, and I like to feel the pressures still on the characters. I almost see the history of the rehearsals in the performance. If I go to see a production that's having a long run I'm interested in its growth, its movement. When I went to see *London Assurance* late on in the run I wrote letters to the actors and a great screed of public notes which were cyclostyled and passed round. Starting with diagnoses of diseases in the production like "creeping anticipation" and giving instances of where it was happening and what questions to ask yourself in order to stop it getting any further. And that's the state in which I usually look at a play I've done. Only on the last night do I sit back and feel a bit complacent. Because it's nearly dying then. Though that's not quite true either. I remember giving a very rough time to an actor who'd just played the last night of *Widowers' Houses* at Stratford East. His way of counting to ten and swallowing his sense of outrage was to walk once around the block. But, as I explained to him when we were both cooler, we might find ourselves collaborating again some day. I certainly wanted to think so – and why didn't we look on that night's crisis and clarifications as the first move in the next job?'

JOHN GIELGUD

'John Gielgud's strongest impulse,' Paul Scofield has said, 'both conscious and instinctive, seems to me to be directed towards form and symmetry, an affirmation of the beauty of language and the perfection of visual line. An impulse which has been responsible for more moments of awareness of beauty than I have found from anyone else in the theatre. His chief weapon is for speaking, which seems in the same instant to search for form and to rest in a civilized certainty. This is his area of total authority, and the tangles of relationship, the psychological inquiry, and the small change of human behaviour have not I think provided material for him as an actor. He will smooth the odd ugly angle into something symmetrical.'

One of the most extraordinary things about Gielgud's career is the variety of the parts he has played in his fifty years on stage, while doing so little to change either his physical appearance or the sound of his voice. Within the limitations of his range he has great suppleness, but his acting does not depend at all on impersonation. Talking in his characteristically self-disparaging way, he says 'I think that really I'm apt to be Richard II or Hamlet or whatever I do, and if you've seen me in those parts and think I've really succeeded in those parts, those parts have seemed to permeate my personality. But you cannot avoid your own particular mannerisms recurring to some extent over the years, though Coquelin is supposed to have altered himself completely in every part he played.'

One characterization in which Gielgud did substantially transform himself, both physically and vocally, was the Shylock in his own 1938 production of *The Merchant of Venice*. Laurence Olivier considers this to be one of the best performances Gielgud has ever given, but the critics were hostile and he became unhappy about it. 'I got very bad notices as

Shylock. I was terribly put down by it, because I thought I'd done it well. There were some beautiful performances and I thought it was a good production, but somehow or other I couldn't find Shylock at all. I thought I had a good make-up. Whether people didn't want to see me in that part, or whether it was because of the Nazis or because I didn't think about it enough I don't know. I do remember that it seemed a very fragmentary part in which you couldn't get very much from the other people. Bassanio and Antonio seemed such stooges in the first scene, and then you have the scene with Tubal, another stooge, the scene with Launcelot and Jessica, and they're stooges, and finally the trial scene, in which I did think I made a great mistake in the staging. Funnily enough I tried to get in that scene rather the same thing that presumably Jonathan Miller achieved in his 1970 production at the National Theatre – making it rather drab and matter of fact. And I had a rather simple set too – white pillars and brown curtains, and Antonio in a funny little dock, and no sort of splendour. And I remember thinking afterwards "Oh what a mad mistake I made". Because I had seen Ellen Terry do it on tour – just the trial scene – with a kind of imitation of the old Lyceum production, with a lot of colour and splendour. And I suddenly thought "I'm sure that Shakespeare must have meant this scene to be very spectacular and splendid." Because it's such high melodrama that if you try and reduce it to hum-drum terms, it doesn't seem to work. It's like destroying the scale of Dickens. It's a very highly coloured scene. In fact I think the whole play is. The old production of Irving probably had a kind of grand old-fashioned ceremony that was very suitable to the play.

'Of course I'm very old-fashioned. I shall never forget seeing Ellen Terry come on in that red dress, on the pier at Brighton, entering with wonderful flowing strides, with a book under her arm. It impressed me tremendously, whether because she was a great actress, or old and famous, and besides that she was actually my great aunt. I believed it all of course, but then I was only twelve. I can't imagine what the scenery was like really. But there was a sort of grandeur about it all. You know if you go to Venice and you've seen the Doge's Palace, you can't really have a little committee room on the stage. Shakespeare must have imagined it even more splendidly than we did, and we all know what the court of Elizabeth was like – gallants sweeping about and all those grand clothes – I don't think you can belittle all that in the theatre. I think you are throwing away such an enormous card in your pack if you do. Not real gondolas or any of that realistic nonsense, but that's where Craig was so marvellous in his drawings for *Venice Preserv'd* and the designs for *Henry V* – there was always a marvellous proportion and space – very simplified, to draw attention to the figures or to the heights or to the contrast of the heights and the figures – not a lot of niggly detail. Also he has big curtains and high doorways that you can come through easily. One only has to look at Venice or even at Hampton Court. You either came in through a tiny door because you were coming out of prison, or you came through great double doors that were flung open, and you walked in as if you were seven foot high. And these mystiques are things that the theatre has cherished and lived on for four or five or six hundred years, and it seems to me rather mad to throw them out. Because there is a way – if you have the right eye and the right designer – to use the essentials of them today without being either cliché or commonplace.'

The unfavourable reaction to his Shylock may have helped to steer Gielgud towards 'straight' rather than 'character' acting in his subsequent career. Reactions to some of previous characterizations that had depended on disguise (like Noah in Michel St Denis's production of Andre Obey's play) had indicated that his public preferred to see him on stage looking like himself.

And in the whole of your career since, you've never disguised yourself in the same way as you did as Noah and Shylock?

'No, I suppose I haven't. Well, in the last few years it's been very unfashionable. We did argue about whether I should wear a moustache or not wear a moustache as Harry in David Storey's *Home* because I didn't wear any make-up or any disguise of any kind. So that it's curiously happened that ever since Enid Bagnold's play *The Last Joke* I haven't had to alter myself in any way really. And I think that has helped one to be more true to oneself. Anyway, I've never thought impersonation to be one of my talents. I think it went well with Noah because that was a tour de force: people were impressed that I could do it at all. When I did half try it in *The Maitlands*, the audience wouldn't take it at all, and I wasn't any good either. I altered myself a bit in *The Cherry Orchard*. With Wolsey after the first night of *Henry VIII*, Michael Benthall said "Oh you made a terrible mistake not to be fat," and at first I had hardly any make-up on, and that wasn't any good. When I put more on and padded my body, I think I was rather more effective. I tried not to play for sympathy, to make him more gross and a little more common. But perhaps you can play Wolsey and get away with it as a sort of High Churchman, except that the public knows more about those parts now than they did in the Irving days. Maybe they did know he was a butcher's son, but they hadn't read all those biographies and details, which the ordinary public now knows about, so I think they would be less likely nowadays to accept an aristocratic Wolsey, which certainly isn't really right. I think Laughton should have played Wolsey rather than Henry VIII. He would have been wonderful.'

There is a point of view from which all acting is just an elaborate game, an adult prolongation of the childish pleasures of dressing up in fine clothes and pretending to be someone else. Occasionally actors halt in their tracks to ask themselves what they have been doing with their lives and whether it has all been worthwhile. But these moments are rare, and most of the time most actors would say, as Gielgud says, 'I can't imagine how one could live otherwise.'

He is interested in the extent to which success depends on ability to concentrate. 'All arts and crafts, like sports, demand enormous concentration, and I've never had good concentration at all, but I do naturally try to concentrate on the one thing I am really interested in. But I've always been very sluggish about training myself to be concentrated. I imagine if you're a clever businessman or golf-player or boxer or cricketer or a dancer, you devote half your life to sheer physical slogging and discipline and training to achieve concentration. We don't have enough of this in the theatre. The ordinary person who isn't an actor learns to concentrate mainly through application. Even a man who sits at a desk or works in a bank. But even when I was in dramatic school I

used to slink out of all the things I didn't like, just as I slunk
out of playing games or swimming at school, and I concentrated on getting out of these irksome things in order to do
other things I wanted to do more. In the same way I avoided
trying to learn fencing or voice production, elocution – all
those things I shirked, because I thought "I can do them my
own way and get away with it." It's quite easy (if you're
fairly sly) to keep working hard, but only at the things you
do most easily, which of course isn't really the way to become
good, unfortunately.'

He was lucky, of course, with what he had inherited – a
Terry voice from his mother's side of the family, and from his
father, an innate musicality, including a gift for playing the
piano by ear. 'I never had any trouble with breathing, and
when people began to tell me I spoke affectedly, I worked hard
to simplify my diction, and to appreciate the phrasing and the
actual shape of sentences and words. I never had any difficulty
with that, but perhaps that's from a musical sense, which I
always had very strongly. It wasn't ever a trouble to me but
a pleasure and, when a thing is pleasure as well as part of your
work, of course you persevere.

'They used to hold my diaphragm and make me do breathing
exercises and I always thought "Oh, nonsense." I showed off
dreadfully in my speaking of verse. In fact that was the great
fault of my acting for a number of years, that I was very vain
about the fact that my diction and my voice were praised and
admired. But then on the other hand I've been told I was inaudible in nearly every part I've played in my life. And I
tell people that and they say "Oh, you are affected, you with
the great silver voice that's heard in the remotest corners of
the earth." And I say "Well if I'm not extremely careful I drop
my voice at the end of sentences like everybody else does."
You've got to be quite cunning to throw your voice in the
theatre so that every word is heard, and I worried for many
years about my self-consciousness and affected way of walking
and standing on the stage.

'I've never played a low-life part – which perhaps is rather
lucky – because I don't think I could ever succeed with accents
or dialects. I haven't a natural gift for mimicry or accents. I've
never even played a Frenchman. I did play with an accent in
something. But I sort of invented it. It wasn't a real accent.

Something I did on the wireless, I think. Or maybe it was in
The Last Joke. I had a sort of accent in Shylock which I
invented for myself. I have never studied accents, and I have
no languages, which is rather a pity because I'm sure I could
have learnt if I'd been forced to. My eldest brother spoke
perfect French. But I have a good accent and I think I could
have spoken French much better than most English people do.
Like Churchill, most Englishmen think it's rather effective to
speak French with a terrible British accent.'

Another gift he always had was a great visual flair. As a
schoolboy he did a good deal of sketching, and at one time the
theatrical career he planned for himself was as a designer. As
a director he has been able to work very closely with his
scenic and costume designers. But as an actor he has had little
help from scenery. 'When I was young I always thought the
scenery would be so helpful. One of the last times I saw Craig
I said in a rather jocose way "Oh I was so disappointed because
I always thought it would be so inspiring to play in front of
wonderful scenery. But of course when one is on the stage
oneself, one never sees the scenery as it is always behind one!"
And he said blandly "Oh my dear boy why don't you have
mirrors put at the back of the theatre? They would reflect the
scenery, and that would inspire you." And I remember that
actually happening in Toronto when I was playing Hamlet
and there were mirrors all the way round the back of the stalls,
and I had to have them all covered up, because I saw five
reflections of myself during the soliloquies, and I couldn't
concentrate at all.

'But if you are a director as well as an actor you do see
the scenery, and the whole picture much more often than
ordinary actors do. Even though one is in front of it when
one is acting, one can still visualize the grouping one has
arranged. As a rule I find that most actors don't rush in front
the moment they aren't in a scene and see what the director is
doing. But I always do, because I am very aware of grouping
and the pattern of the play from the front. And this way I
feel I know better how to fit my own performance in when I
join the other actors.'

Another inherited gift was the ability to shed tears at will.
Weeping comes so easily to him that often he has to restrain
it. 'In Gordon Daviot's *Richard of Bordeaux*, in the last scene

of self-sacrifice, the less I gave way to tears myself, the more moved the audience was. Ellen Terry is said to have been able to play the fool for the other actors' benefit even while she was openly weeping her way through a pathetic scene. My mother was, like all her family, extremely emotional as an audience or when reading aloud, though – as I am, too – surprisingly stoical in life during an emergency or emotional crisis. In Shakespeare especially, as was the case with Ellen Terry, I've always had difficulty in restraining easy tears, both in the voice and the eyes, but the deliberate use of this ability, properly controlled – after a certain amount of over-indulgence at rehearsals, and sometimes in performance too – has been of great value to me in parts like Hamlet, Leontes and Richard II, in the scene with the priest in Graham Greene's *The Potting Shed*, in *Home* and once or twice even in comedy parts like the Headmaster in Alan Bennett's *40 Years On*, when a sudden moment of real feeling was required. But audiences are inclined to be over-impressed with actors who really weep; when I once said to Edith Evans "I've learnt exactly the word to start weeping on and the word to stop weeping on," she said "Ah, you're learning to be a good actor". She never milks a scene herself, but in *The Chalk Garden* and in *The Late Christopher Bean*,* she opens the shutters and shows you her heart – then closes them again quickly before she can over-indulge the emotions either of herself or the audience.

'Edith Evans has influenced me a lot. The audience may influence her timing but she resists any temptation to woo them. She moves very little. Even as Millamant she managed to give the impression of a fascinating coquette without much gesture or movement, so that her few moments of action were the more significant.'

Like her, Gielgud has given many of his best performances in classical comedy – Shakespeare, Congreve, Sheridan and Wilde. Here the technical knowledge that he has acquired as a director has been inseparable from his achievements as an actor. One of his greatest comedy successes was as Joseph Surface in Tyrone Guthrie's 1937 production of *The School for Scandal*, though this got off to a very bad start on the first night. 'I remember that I sort of pawed the ground and

*An adaptation by Emlyn Williams of René Fauchois's *Prenez garde à la peinture*.

went on, and then a terrible thing happened. I dried up on my very first line, and had to take it from the prompter. I was terribly nervous and my mind was a complete blank. It's the only time it's happened to me in the theatre, so I was in a frenzy. I had a beautiful costume, I looked very good and I think the few things Guthrie had said to me were rather helpful, and I made the hypocritical Joseph agreeable and rather attractive. The production was quite a success, although I thought a lot of it was very misguided. *The Times* rightly said that the curtain call looked as if we had all gone to the Russian Ballet, and actually it was more carefully rehearsed than anything else in the play. There was an enormous sofa Guthrie had got from some great house and we all bounced up and down on it. This got a lot of laughs, but killed the dialogue. I had a very strong sense then in that play, and later in *The Importance of Being Earnest*, and in *Much Ado* and in *Love for Love*, that in comedy the distance of people on the stage from one another is one of the vital things. And it's something that must have changed very much, because in the days of candle lighting, everybody had to play very much dead front. It does depend enormously on how the furniture is placed, how wide the stage is, and how much ground you have to cover when you move and when you keep still. All this affects the way that comedy is flung from one character to the other and the way one player feeds and the other takes.

'When I was brought in to direct *The Heiress**** at the last minute – which was a great moment for me, to gain the confidence of a very depressed company of actors very late in rehearsals – I realized at once that the man who had preceded me as director had completely missed the point about those rather sententious Henry James scenes, in which it was essential that people sat on the stage and talked at a certain distance from one another, either close or far. But if they were standing throughout a scene of talk, you felt they were in a sort of waiting-room, that at any moment they'd rush off stage to catch a train, and the audience simply couldn't listen.

'In *The School for Scandal*, it's obvious that the scandal scenes are meant to be played on small chairs and sofas from which people simply throw the ball from one to another across the stage. But if everyone is crowded together, as we were in

*An adaptation by Ruth and Augustus Goetz of Henry James's *Washington Square*.

Guthrie's production, on a big settee, cheek by jowl, you can't convey a real effect of witty conversation or give the audience breathing space to be amused by it. In a real party it's very important how you sit with people. If you're talking intimately, or if you're talking to amuse a crowd, if you're being witty, in a circle or at a dinner table, then the *placement* is very important. I always remember Lady Cunard. When I dined with her at the end of the war at the Dorchester she used to have a big round table and put eight or ten people round it, but I noticed the tremendous care she took in placing the guests. A clever hostess knows where the wittiest person should sit and where he's going to dominate best. And which man and which woman on the right of him are going to be the best balance for one another to get the conversation going.'

Gielgud's habit of wandering out into the auditorium during the rehearsal of other actors' scenes stood him in good stead during the nerve-wracked rehearsals of David Storey's *Home* in 1970. 'We felt so exposed sitting at the front of the stage at that table all through that long opening scene. And then I saw the scene in the second act between Ralph and Dandy Nichols from the front, and realised at once, sitting in the auditorium, that there was a kind of third dimension the moment I was away from it, of which playing on the stage I was completely unaware.

'This discovery immediately gave one more confidence. I didn't feel so bare and desperate, or that the scenes wouldn't hold. Lindsay Anderson had done wonders with the few moments of movement in the play. In the last scene, after I had sat between the two women and the table had been taken away, I came down a few steps to the front and Ralph went up to the back, the effect was very striking, though it was impossible for the actors to judge that for themselves. We just had to move as the director told us. I've had battles sometimes with actors and actresses when I've been directing them, because they didn't want to move on a certain line, or they wanted to sit down on a certain line, and in a conventional play the actor has a very strong instinct about that. But in a new kind of play like *Home*, although we continually did say "Can I stay still so long? Can I get up?" the director invented all of the moves, of which there were very few, and he once said towards the middle of rehearsals "Don't ever move on your instincts. When you feel you want to move on a certain line, always delay it. Either do it a little before or a little after, because it gives this kind of oblique suggestion of not being quite right in the head. Don't move on a line as you would in a conventionally constructed play in which you're going to make a point."

'I was very worried when he said "Now don't listen to the others, turn your back and look at the sky". I said "Won't it kill the points that they're making in the front of the stage?" Because one's whole training as an actor is never to move when somebody else has got a good line. And no one else must move when you have a good line. In Storey's play we could break all the old rules, and it was terribly interesting, but you had to trust the director that it would be all right, not disturbing. There was so little movement that any move was noticeable and important. I had to cross the stage several times right in front of the characters who were speaking, which I would never have presumed to do in another kind of play. In a formal play or in Shakespeare it's absolutely essential that you don't draw attention to yourself at the wrong moment. In *Home* everything was so compact and there were so few of us that it was essential to keep the shape and balance and tone exactly.

'What I liked so much about Jocelyn Herbert's set for *Home* was that it had the beauty of a Craig without his tendency to dwarf the actors. It was wonderfully simple and that white light was splendid too. In Peter Shaffer's *The Battle of Shrivings* and in *Home* we played under strong white lights – pretty trying when we had to look into them all the time. But the actors were lit superbly. Until ten years ago all actors demanded footlights. Alfred Lunt and Lynne Fontanne wouldn't appear without them. On tour they even took a set of footlights along with them in case they weren't otherwise available. Women always wanted Surprise Pink in the lights because they believed it made them look younger. Now we wear no make-up, there are no footlights and we have blinding white light which throws no shadows. Hours I used to spend in theatres when I was directing, trying to get shadows away from the backcloth. I've sat twelve hours in a theatre trying to light a play, because I don't really know anything about it technically and I had to do it by trial and error. But in *Shrivings* and *Home*, which were marvellously set and lit, there was hardly any change of lighting during the performance. What an enormous revolution in every department has come about in the last ten years!'

'Well this is Brecht's influence. He used open white light.'

'Yes, I remember it very well when I saw *Trumpets and Drums* in Berlin in 1955. Of course in the old days you always lit your play yourself if you were the director. Komisarjevsky was a great master of lighting – I learned much from him. Now a lighting expert is nearly always specially engaged and even at the Court there is a lighting box at the back of the auditorium. All the modern theatres, schools, as well as the Vic and Stratford, have now got lights not only on the stage and at the front of the house, but also a lighting box in which the operator sits, in touch with the prompt corner. So between the two you can pretty well ensure that no serious mistake is made. So that the technicians can see and correct at once any mistakes that are made. In the old days, on tour, you would have to relight your production every time the play moved to another provincial city. You would go on to a big scene in a Shakespeare play, and the important light wasn't on, and you were playing in pitch darkness, and nobody on the lighting board could see what was missing. There's a famous story of Alec Guinness in his *Hamlet* at the New. They had put in a new Pre-set board the day before, which went wrong on the first night, and every cue worked one cue late. So that in the first scene, it was bright daylight for the night scene and then for Claudius's court it was pitch dark. No ordinary lay person realizes what disastrous effect it has if the stage management and lighting should fail.'

Gielgud was full of admiration for Lindsay Anderson's work on *Home*, particularly over the cutting. 'I wouldn't have had the faintest idea what to cut, and he finally cut, I think, nearly ten minutes. Storey was very very quiet, and Lindsay would say "I think these three lines should come out." They're such little lines, and they're all so tenuous, and one would think it wouldn't much matter if this line came out or that line, or you didn't say "Oh yes" for the tenth time. But Lindsay seemed to know exactly how long each passage would sustain without becoming boring. Quite a lot of very good jokes were lost but I think the cuts were exactly right. The play is beautifully short. Of course silly people said to me "It's lovely, but why can't you have a part that gives you more opportunity to speak?"

'You can never please audiences completely. They prefer you to be the way they liked you before. I've come to the conclusion that there is a great nostalgia in audiences – especially with middle-aged people. As they themselves get older, they don't want us to get older on the stage because we reflect for them their own youth and enthusiasm. And when we come on looking as old as they are, without make-up, without disguise, without any panache, and in a "failure" part like the men in *Home*, or like Chekhov's Ivanov, they're apt to be disappointed. They go to the theatre to see us restore their taste for romance and sympathy and poetic abandon and emotion. And if one no longer plays that kind of part, however good they may think you, they're slightly disappointed. On the other hand you may be making a new public of younger people, who perhaps would never have liked you in your old romantic roles.

'*The Ages of Man** got rid of much of my romantic past. And *Home* was a marvellous chance. I can't imagine any of the actors of Ralph's and my standing being offered a play like this (or accepting it) even twenty years ago. Olivier did a great service to the Establishment actor by going to the Royal Court in John Osborne's *The Entertainer* and Scofield afterwards in *Vanya*. I don't suppose the Court would have offered *Home* to Ralph and me unless they'd had those actors to play there, because they would think we wouldn't be interested enough to take less money and appear in this kind of play. Of course we were both afraid of making a mess of it and spoiling our reputations. Neither of us were sure which of the two men's parts we should agree to take. Tony Richardson, who'd read it very quickly and was wild about it, said to me "I think you ought to read both parts and see which one comes out the best for you". But I hardly liked to suggest this. So I said to Ralph "Well which part?" He said "Well I want to do the one with the conjuring tricks". And I said "All right, fine. Then I'll play the other one". And although I'd read the play a couple of times I didn't yet realize how frightfully terse my

*A one-man show based on George Rylands's Shakespeare anthology.

part was. And when we had the first reading, and he had a good many fairly long speeches and I had nothing but monosyllables to answer, I thought "I must be mad, I'm going to be the poor old stooge. There's no part at all, perhaps I ought to give it up". And then Ralph got frightfully depressed too and said "I think *I* ought to give it up, I don't think this play is strong enough". We had fearful doubts, and Lindsay Anderson kept very quiet and so did Storey, though they must have seen us going through all these alarming doubts. We both felt that after a week we could still retire gracefully without causing too much havoc, and they could get somebody else. Of course, until we knew it, we couldn't act it. We stumbled along, saying our strange lines over and over again. I think it was very trusting of us, because you see we were all old stagers – the two actresses felt the same. And it was very clever of the director to produce enough confidence in us to get over that first bridge of acute suspicion which we all had with such an unusual text.

'It's a marvellous invention when at the opening of the second act the boy comes on and wrestles with the table. So strikingly physical after the stillness and quietness of the whole of the first act. And the way the furniture is gradually moved away to make the feeling of everything being taken away from the characters towards the end.'

There was a great deal about the play that the actors could not understand. 'We kept on asking Storey about the background. "What does this refer to?" And we kept on inventing our own reasons for things we mentioned that seemed to have no specific bearing on the play. For instance I say, looking off-stage, "Eyes in the back of your head. Won't do that again in a hurry, will he?" And Ralph answers "I had an uncle once who bred horses." Ralph had the idea that there was really a horse that kicked someone, off-stage. Well, you can't be sure of conveying that to the audience, but it was fun to think of it. Because it gave us a reason for saying it. But Storey wouldn't explain. He said "Well perhaps that's it". He wouldn't commit himself. And the difficulty was that everything we had to say could be either fact or fantasy, and neither we nor the audience, nor the characters themselves really knew for certain. So we had to invent a secret life for ourselves and it was no good discussing it, because it was private to each character. Some of the jokes in the play are splendid. They're tender, not witty but just charming, like *Alice in Wonderland* jokes.'

Do you find yourself varying much in performance?

'I'm determined not to vary. I don't think I do any more, I'm proud of myself, because ever since *Measure for Measure* at Stratford in 1950, I started to discipline myself and not experiment as I always used to do. And ever since then I've really prided myself that I don't add very much or put in very much or take out very much. I simplify as much as possible. Of course you do play better when the audience is with you. You like them to laugh. Not too much. You need the laughter as a softening, a mellowing. But I never cared in *Home* or in Chekhov plays whether they laughed or applauded or cried. I played much more with the fourth wall down in those plays. And for once, although I dreaded it so in Seneca's *Oedipus* and in *40 Years On*, I found looking out at the house very easy in *Home*. Lindsay said at the beginning "Don't turn your back, don't use the ensemble actor's technique of playing together. Play out. Live your life alone through the play." I found that was not so difficult as I'd feared. And sitting in a relaxed way. I've always *sat* on a stage with a tremendously straight back and my legs stretched out, and used a sort of athletic attack that's always been very tiring. But in the Storey play in a small theatre I learned to relax my body, and concentrate with my mind. It was very much less physically exhausting, and that alone, as one gets older, is rather a relief – not to have to put on make-up, not to have to change your clothes, not to have to play violent scenes in which you're breathless and sweating and exhausted at the end. And to know that by being very quiet you're still holding an audience. And using one's voice realistically but not theatrically. I said "How am I going to say 'Well I . . . Well I . . .' fifty times? If I'm to begin planning set tones and inflections for every repetition, then in a few days it's going to become a terrible sort of gramophone record". Lindsay said "Don't decide how you're going to do it. It'll come out right. Do it like Chopin. It's very flexible". And once I had managed to learn the cues correctly I found I didn't worry. I don't prepare how I'm going to speak. There were a few passages towards the end of the play in which the men had to echo each other. Those

I did grade very carefully, vocally, because I knew they must have a very good crescendo, my voice being higher than Ralph's. Such things we planned very accurately, but for the general trend of the give and take, I just emptied my mind and tried to live my character, and Richardson did the same. We never seemed to fail to contrast each other properly.

'We all tried not to imagine all the time we were mad or to think of eccentric things to do. I did put in a slightly off-beat walk, crossing the paving stones rather oddly. This I was terrified by over-elaborating. But as I've spent all my life trying to stride gracefully across the stage, I thought "If I do this slightly hesitating thing with my feet it should give a valuable effect of slight uncertainty". So I invented my walk fairly late on in rehearsals. And in that tiny theatre you could do so little, that everything made its mark.

What about Oedipus? *Did that vary much?*

'Yes I think it did – the whole production as well as individual performances, even though we had ten weeks rehearsal. It was a very unpredictable and variable emotional experience – just as *Noah* was so many years ago. Almost impossible to play either well, except for one or two rare performances. Some nights they used to say I was very good. All the preparatory work had been agony, and misery, and I really resented it in some sort of way, except that I love Peter Brook, and I always have a feeling that anything you do which you resent in the way of preparation – like learning how to use a billiard cue, or learning languages, or doing exercises – the very fact that you hate doing it must mean that it's rather good discipline and may possibly lead to something good. Like going into training or going on a diet or not smoking or drinking. One's often had one's own way too much and to be forced to make an effort is valuable. I think all the physical work improved my balance and control. There again we never quite knew what Peter was driving at . . . He never showed us models of the set or decided till the last moment what costumes we were to wear. And it wasn't until the whole thing was together and we had the set, the lights and the chorus deployed round the front of the circles. We did weeks of very fascinating exercises, in which I showed up pretty badly. And that was good for me too, because the company was a very young one and I made a bit of a fool of myself, which I think increased their respect for me. But also decreased my respect for myself and made me feel that I could afford to make a fool of myself in front of them all without lowering my prestige. One had to risk looking idiotic, which most leading players avoid at all costs. So as not to be found out. Feet of clay and all that. But the work reduced us all to the same level, which was of great value to me, I think, in the end.

'When I went into *40 Years On* soon afterwards, I had to play in a very relaxed and intimate way, aware of the audience nearly all the time. This would once have terrified me, but I found it comparatively easy, to my great surprise, and attributed my relaxation to the strict discipline of the *Oedipus* work with Brook, which had somehow broken down many of my personal mannerisms and self-consciousness.'

The art of acting is the art of making transitions. To speak a single line arrestingly is nothing: any drama student can do it. A good actor is no more interesting in the effects he achieves than in the connections he builds between them. One of the director's main functions in rehearsal is to help him to avoid clichés in bridging from one thought or feeling to the next. And sometimes within an individual speech. With an actor like Gielgud, few directors have the courage or the ability to be really helpful. 'When you get past a certain point in your career, the trouble is that everyone is too respectful to tell you about your faults. That's why I like Peter Brook and Lindsay Anderson so much. They are never rude but they do tell you. When actors get older, they find it hard, of course, to think of new ways of making transitions. You need someone with a very keen eye who can tell you "I don't want any of those old tricks you've used before".'

Another disadvantage of success is the knowledge that one's mannerisms have become popular. So it becomes a temptation to fall back on them rather than think one's way to a new and difficult transition. 'I think your mannerisms are often what audiences like best. They also help to sustain the agony of repetition. Because you can rely on effects which come very naturally to you as signposts in your performance: " I do this bit here. I put on my tears or I put on my heroic voice. And this will help you to carry the next passage through". You take refuge in what you know will appeal and be effective. Every actor must make certain effects. But the danger is of allowing effects to dominate you, to allow them to become more important than your truths. The "effect" of acting, like the "effect" of painting or anything else, must be something you produce on yourself to make the audience convinced. But if it becomes too consciously a trick, it's apt to become a debit rather than an asset.

'Of course you're always on show, but so you are in life as well. When you go to a party, you can't quite be sure when you're being truthful. I fancy that without knowing it I always study my behaviour in private life for the benefit of my work in the theatre. In quarrels and rages, even in great sorrow or delight, I cannot resist watching all the time to see what I'm doing. I see the stage possibilities in every emotion, situation, conversation. But aren't we all manqué actors? A great hostess or a great diplomat or a great speaker in the House of Commons – they're all speaking what they want to speak but at the same time judging their effects. Shaw must have been tremendous like that. In an after-dinner speech one always tries to cover with spontaneous charm what one hasn't really studied to say. And in interviews and radio talks and television talks I think the only thing to trust to is your own sincerity. But how sincere you really are is a terrible uncertainty, above all to yourself. You try to be sincere, but without knowing it, you colour your words according to the people who are interviewing you, according to the audience you think you're speaking to. Because you've had great experience of dominating an audience, with somebody else's words, and now you have to use your own.'

As a director, Gielgud is notorious for wanting to alter everything he established the previous day. As Peggy Ashcroft has complained, 'He's maddening as a director of course, setting things one day in one way and then the next day arriving and saying "Wouldn't it be fun to try it like this?" I never agreed with him. In fact I could never understand why he wanted to go on using me. And it was years before I had the feeling in a part "Here is something firm that I can hold on to". He's an inspirational director. And an inspirational actor, of course.'

Irene Worth defends his directorial habits. 'I think it's poky and old-fashioned to resent the way he changes his mind in rehearsal. It's right to explore all the possibilities there are, and he finds it refreshing to his imagination. He has tremendous stamina and energy, and he actually requires less physical rest than most people do.'

But Edith Evans found it very distressing, when she was asked to alter what she had been developing. 'I get terribly upset when he wants to change things half-way through rehearsals. Because I've given him what came out of my heart. What the Almighty gave me as a way of earning my living. And when something is half-way there, it's like a child. You can't say "It's not a boy now, it's a girl".'

Harry Andrews says 'I only once lost my temper with him and that was when he tried to make a radical change in my characterization at a very late rehearsal. I stamped my foot and shouted at him. "You know you really can't do that to me. You know I'm not an actor who can take such big changes at the last minute". "Oh yes, Harry, I'd quite forgotten. You are rather slow".'

Ralph Richardson claims to have found the right way of coping with the ceaseless flow of new ideas he has always had from Gielgud over the forty years they have so frequently worked together. 'Directors often think they're found a way to manage actors. I think I've found a way to manage a director, and the way I've worked so happily over so many years with Johnny G. is to pin him down. Johnny's rather like a catherine wheel. He springs out with a thousand ideas. Many of them are extremely valuable and I think I'm rather a good editor for them. He'll say "You come through the door and you go straight up to the chair and you sit down". The next day he'll say "I think you should come down the chimney and you should go up to the window and go out of it". I say "Now Johnny, you gave me a marvellous idea yesterday. I'm not going to change that idea until you give me a better one". Out of this catherine wheel I have a little bit of the skill to find and retain the best of the things he gives, and it adds up to something.'

Until 1972, the last play Gielgud had directed in London was Peter Ustinov's *Half Way up the Tree* in 1967, so he was very pleased, while playing in *Home* on Broadway in 1970, to be offered the new Albee play, *All Over*. "I thought it would be fascinating to do it and I had a very interesting time with the four fine actresses who played the leading parts. The actual writing of the speeches all through the play is very fine and I enjoyed phrasing it, and moving it, and I had no movement at all, except when it was absolutely necessary. Everyone sat facing the audience on enormous pieces of furniture and just spoke the play. Albee was very pleased with that. I thought it worked very well but the house was too big and people couldn't hear. We had a fortnight of previews, which were full, and very controversial, just as they were in *Tiny Alice*. And then no-one came. The cast went on cut salaries after a week and the play only ran three more weeks.'

Putting himself into the hands of a new director, as he did with Robin Phillips for *Caesar and Cleopatra* at Chichester, Gielgud can be pliable and trusting, though he cannot limit himself to thinking about his own part. His mind flies up to take a director's, even a historian's view of the play and the playwright. *Caesar and Cleopatra* interested him particularly as being the first play to put modern colloquial dialogue into the mouths of famous historical characters. He sees *Richard of Bordeaux* and *Vivat! Vivat Regina!* as being 'in direct succession' to it. 'Shaw was the most marvellous instrumentalist, vocally. He knew exactly how a speech should be turned. He was such a good public speaker himself. Where Phillips was very good with one was that he checked me when I learned the speeches too glibly and phrased them well musically but recited them for their own content and not really to inform the other characters. I found that more difficult to do on an open stage than it would be on a picture stage. Where one might be sitting close or just apart from someone on two chairs or at a table, there we were with this big stage to throw the lines across and sometimes we even had to speak without looking at the person we were talking to, coming down to the front of the stage and looking out over the audience and speaking as it were over our shoulders, without turning. It made the intimate scenes very difficult to play, because one couldn't get too close to anybody. Caesar was anyway a difficult part because it has quite a lot of gags and a strong comedy twist to it, and yet he must never fail to convince the audience that he really is a great man.'

Nearly thirty years previously, in 1943, Shaw had written to Gielgud, trying to woo him away from *Love for Love*

at the Haymarket to star in the film of *Caesar and Cleopatra*.
'You will have to play Caesar some day,' he wrote, 'just as you
have had to play Hamlet and Macbeth. You owe him to your
repertory.' But Gielgud didn't take this very seriously. 'I must
have been awfully stupid. I think I was so contemptuous of the
possibilities of films, and I'd always had a sort of idea that I
didn't find anything in Shaw that appealed to me very much.
And in 1943 I'd have been too young and in 1971 I was too
old.'

Of course the fact of working on an open stage made it impossible to observe Shaw's stage directions. 'Robin got rather
impatient with the endless and rather spectacular stage directions.
He maintained that Shaw's colour sense must have been at fault,
that he must have been colour blind. He was such a brilliant
auditory man but, judging by the things he seemed to admire
in the stage directions, everything ought to be purple and gold
and great shadows, everything rather Royal Academy. Of
course this was the Edwardian theatre taste, and probably he
wrote the stage directions to please Forbes-Robertson.* But I
wonder what Shaw's own pictorial taste was like. I think he
liked the portraits of himself by Topolski and Epstein but I
don't fancy he had much feeling for modern pictures. And of
course in 1898 the whole thing was conceived to be – you
know – Joseph Harker scenery with enormous gods and masses
of extras. We tried to simplify it. Robin had seized very
much on the idea of an old man creating a woman out of a
little girl – which was, I think, very good, as this girl, Anna
Calder-Marshall, is so suited to it, being so small. She really
looks like a little girl, almost completely asexual, which I'm
sure is what Shaw intended, with Ftatateeta as a Nanny. The
attitudes are Edwardian – the images of childhood and the
mastery in Caesar are basically the Edwardian approach of
children to their fathers. Which is exactly what Shaw must
have felt. In a way the play is a first cousin to *Peter Pan*,
which has an Edwardian jokeyness which we find hard to
accept. It's interesting that Shaw, who never had children—
and nor did Barrie either – could understand this child Cleopatra so well, but that he should have thought of it for Mrs
Campbell or Ellen Terry is so peculiar. Because they were
obviously clever grown-up women. But maybe his attitude

*Who played Caesar and co-directed with Shaw.

towards women was very much more the attitude of a teacher
and a father figure than a lover, with his vegetarianism and
Jaeger underwear. He couldn't ever have been very attractive
physically though he was obviously very fascinating. I think at
that time the elder generation had a kind of sedate glamour
which modern young people don't find attractive about us old
people at all.'

NOËL COWARD

Noël Coward had a huge influence on a whole generation. He came of age at the beginning of the twenties but he had been on the stage since childhood and his first play to be produced, a melodrama called *The Last Trick*, was written in 1918. He was the young theatrical lion of the post-war generation, and in 1925 he had five shows, including a revue, running simultaneously in London. Fashionable young men growing up into the twenties vied with each other in assiduous imitation of his laconic charm, his elaborate casualness, his imperturbable and slightly bored sophistication. He was in great demand at parties and his presence was felt almost equally at the ones he did not attend. His songs were sung, his plays were discussed and above all his style was cultivated.

There was as close a connection as ever between fashion in society and theatrical fashion, so John Gielgud was only one of many young actors who found that one of the main problems was how to avoid imitating Coward. But for Gielgud the temptation was quite irresistible, particularly when he understudied Coward in *The Vortex* in 1925, taking over the part later in the year, with Coward's inflections still ringing in his ears. The following year, in *The Constant Nymph*, he again had to take over a leading part which Coward had created, and though he fought hard to be different, he was forming habits which were to affect characterizations he created himself. As late as 1932, when Coward saw him in *Musical Chairs*, the same thing seemed to be happening. 'I went round to him and said "Listen, stop doing this. You're the touring rights of me. Stop it." I had a few mannerisms, which I still have, I presume. I hear it when anybody imitates me. I can't imitate myself very well. And he'd got them all, and was parading them around. And I said "Don't. Get away from me. Think of someone quite different. Godfrey Tearle for instance. Or Martin Harvey."

'You see I came first among all that lot, and I was the belle of the ball, and obviously imitable. And he was giving an extremely bad imitation of me. Again. It was really a very bad performance, and then he was absolutely sweet and changed it and got much better. I didn't very much like the play but that was beside the point.' (It is possible that Gielgud's performance was affected that evening by nervousness, because he had seen Coward sitting in the stalls.) But there was no one who could have made Coward nervous by sitting within view. 'Brashness' is the word he uses to describe the self-confidence he remembers having right from the beginning. 'If someone I admire tremendously is in front, I'm delighted. In my mind I play the whole performance for them and hope they like it. Other people say "Don't let me know—don't let me know". Well I like it – it makes a change. But then you see I've never been shy, and I've never been nervous.'

In classical parts of course there was less danger of imitation, and Coward was full of admiration for Gielgud's Shakespeare, particularly the Hamlet at the Old Vic in 1930 and the Romeo he alternated with Olivier in 1935. 'It was extraordinary because they were both marvellous and absolutely different. Larry was more robust and Johnny more lyrical, I suppose. But they were both wonderful. I wouldn't have known which to choose.'

Their characterizations of Hamlet contrasted in much the same ways. 'John had the lyric quality, which is essential, and Larry had the dramatic quality – he was stronger – which was also essential. I think John's first Hamlet was pretty bloody marvellous, because he was so young, it was so fresh. Larry's was brilliant but more calculated. But then Larry is a much more calculating actor. I have the proud boast of actually stopping Larry giggling on the stage. Because he was *the* worst giggler. If in *Private Lives* I did something different, I'd look across the stage and he'd be in fits, ruining the play; so I finally got very cross with him and said "Listen, from now on I'm going to try to make you laugh, I'm deliberately doing it and I put you on your honour – if you laugh I'll murder you." And I invented a terrible dog called Roger and I used to go up to him in the big quarrel scene and say "Roger, don't do that to those people. Roger! All over the carpet! You've ruined those roses!" And Larry used to collapse, gulp and go purple, and then he got furious with himself and stopped laughing. Then took to making everyone else laugh and ruined *their* performances.

'I think Larry's an extraordinary creature. Not as gentle as John, not as modest, but a very, very great actor – I think the greatest actor I ever saw. When I think of the variety of plays I've seen him in! Do you remember *The Green Bay Tree*?* Larry played that in New York and he was sensational. With him in it it was a completely different play. He did something really extraordinary. Larry suggested that the young man being kept – he wasn't really queer but quite enjoyed it – had virility. And when he crumpled up, it was marvellous, an extraordinary performance.

'I remember him coming round to me when I was playing *The Astonished Heart*. I was acting my lungs out and doing it splendidly, I thought. Everyone was saying how glorious I was – they always do – but he waited behind and said "What are you doing all that stuff for?" And I said "What do you *mean*?" He said "Look, you've got the story, you've got the character, what more do you want? What are you *acting* for? You oughtn't to be acting for a minute". And really ticked me off. And I was very impressed and called a rehearsal for the next morning and found out that I was going overboard. But he could always say anything he liked to me and I could say anything I liked to him – I ticked him off several times. His first Macbeth – oh dear – at Manchester, that was the worst Macbeth I've ever seen in my life, perfectly appalling. Then I saw it two or three years later at Stratford and it was the greatest Macbeth I've ever seen in my life. That I think is fabulous – to make that change. Because not a shred of the original faults remained. In the first one he was self-pitying, and weepy and wailing and awful, tremulo drawn-out cries and all that. In the second he was absolutely marvellous – great.'

Some of Coward's most valuable experience in controlling an audience was gained by performing songs for the troops. 'Once I was very nervous, but then I had every reason – I was singing

*This was the first play to be staged dealing explicitly with a homosexual relationship.

150

to five thousand troops, in the open air, in Assam, next to a shunting yard. I had a wonderful cockney dresser, Bert, and I sang my opening medley to this terrible noise going on – bang, clank, crash – and no-one paying any attention, all the soldiers talking, it was absolutely ghastly. I came off, and Bert said "What the fucking hell do you think you're doing? You're fuckin' up your whole performance. Go out there. Stop 'em. Keep 'em quiet. Giving in?" St George and the dragon I was, then I got 'em by the end of the evening – but it took quite a time. I ruined the first six numbers. If ever you want to learn the hard way, sing to troops. They can be occasionally wonderful, but as a rule they're buggers. Particularly in transit camps. They're either going back to the front line having been on leave, and therefore so miserable that nothing you do can amuse them. Or else going home on leave and so excited they can't pay any attention to you at all. So you're stuck between the two and to keep their attention is really very hard. I was only once booed off. But that was all right. I realized why later. It was in the open-air, and I went out and couldn't see anyone there at all – *anyone*. The reason I couldn't see anybody was that they were absolutely coal black. They were all negroes. Singing "Surrey with the Fringe on Top" and "I'll see you again" to an audience composed entirely of negroes wasn't exactly tactful, was it? So they booed. So I thought "Get off, don't stay here, dear, or you'll have something thrown at you". So I jumped the whole programme to get to my last number. I had a very good finisher which was Cole Porter's "Let's Do It". It was very quick and they had to lean forward a bit to listen to that. They didn't pay much attention, but at least they leaned forward, and once they lean forward you're all right. I sang it so fast that as I went off, finally, sweating, I just caught a glimpse of one poor man, who was rather old, I think he was a General or something, and he obviously hadn't understood one word – I'd been singing so fast to get through it. The great thing to do when you haven't got them is to drop your voice; they think they're missing something, and then they lean forward. Speak very fast and drop your voice – that's the way to get their attention. Once you've got it, you can do what you like.

'When we were small-part actors Edith Evans and I played together a lot. We used to walk home together. She lived in

Pimlico and I lived in Ebury Street, and we used to discuss theatre exhaustively. She used to say about laughs "Throw them away in the first act, dear, pull 'em in the last". It's very true. She knew her oats, our Ede, but she drove me mad when I directed her. She didn't learn her lines. " I can't learn that way. I have to grow with the part". I said "Listen dear, we haven't got much time for you to go on growing". I would like to be able to say she came on the first night and gave the most brilliant performance of her career. Not at all. She buggered up the whole play, and everyone prompted her in unison, the whole cast. That was in Manchester, and we toured for six weeks, but she even dried up on the opening night in London. But she said – which is no way to curry favour with me – "I never learn my words". On the other hand, when I arrive at the first rehearsal, I am virtually word perfect in the whole play. Because it takes me a good three or four weeks rehearsal to decide *how* to do it. The words are the first thing you get out of the way. If you use props to remember something by – and the property man doesn't put them out one night – you're thrown for six. It's a very dangerous way of learning words. And that was Edith's way. And if the chair wasn't in the right place, she'd fluff and have to be prompted. I think that's terrible. People all have their own methods, but then I was brought up by Charles Hawtrey, and I've never done a first rehearsal with a book in my hand. Except as a gesture to the others. I've held it, but I've known it.

'But you must remember I have a quick mind and I'm a quick study. Some actors have very slow minds and are very slow studies. Lynne Fontanne – who was the slowest study of all – Alfred Lunt and I, at the first rehearsal of *Design for Living*, played the whole first act through without fluffing once. The company nearly had a fit. They rushed home, had hysterics, had to have Horlicks and study all night long. We weren't so good in the second and third acts, but still . . .'

Coward readily admits that the best parts in his plays are the ones he wrote for himself. He describes Charles in *Blithe Spirit* as a 'beastly part'. 'There are only two parts in *Blithe Spirit*, Madam Arkati and Elvira; Charles and Ruth trudge through the sludge and hold up the whole play. They have to provide the plot. As I found to my cost when I played it. If

I'd written that part for myself it would have been a better part. But I never realized it until I played it.'

After the parts he wrote for himself, the best ones were written for Gertrude Lawrence. 'No-one ever spoke my comedy lines like Gertie. She had a special thing. I wrote *Private Lives* for us both, in the Café Hotel in Shanghai, and now there's a *plaque* on the door! I found that when I went back years later. I sent her the script, very pleased with myself, because I thought it was very funny and that she'd be delighted: I had a cable back saying *"Read script nothing wrong that can't be fixed"*. So I wrote back "The only thing that's going to be fixed is your performance". She's always maintained since that she meant she was getting out of another contract, which may have been true, but it was an unfortunate way of putting it. She was of course one of my earliest theatre playmates. She was absolutely incredible. She was like mercury – so terribly quick, too quick, and would overact at the drop of a hat. I had to hit her on the head ever Tuesday, which she never resented. I never knew her do an unkind thing or be a bitch in any way. But she used to drive me round the bend. I remember I used to go to the theatre at night, sometimes saying "Please God don't let her do anything awful tonight because I don't feel up to it". She'd do anything to get a laugh, you know. I remember in *We Were Dancing* when she was wearing a white satin Molyneux dress and looking so glamorous and we were singing a song while we were dancing – she was singing to Joyce Carey and I was singing to Alan Webb, and while I was singing I heard an enormous laugh and I thought "What's happened?" And after the play was over I followed Joyce upstairs and said "What happened?" and Joyce, who was the gentlest of creatures, went scarlet in the face and went into her room and slammed the door. And I thought "Oy oy oy – something very bad". So the next night I turned round and the way Gertie was getting a laugh – quite simple, she just stuck practically her whole hand up her bottom – in a white satin Molyneux dress and a romantic comedy. And that, not unnaturally, got a laugh.

'Oh, I absolutely gave her hell! And she said "But wasn't it better?" So I said "No dear, it wasn't better, it was fucking awful. Why did you do it?" She said "Oh well it got a laugh". I said "You'd also get a laugh by pulling a kipper out of your twat but it wouldn't quite be in the romantic vein, would it?" But she was a darling.'

Another comedy actress Coward liked to work with was Yvonne Arnaud. 'I adored Yvonne. She was always right. She would take a line in a play and say "I'll get a titter on that line, which I must kill. I'll get a laugh on that one – not big enough to matter – I must kill it so as to get to this one". She went through the script like that with a pencil, writing down what she was going to do, and what she was *going* to do she did. She was a marvellous comedienne, she knew how to time.'

Theatrical fashion has turned against this kind of approach to performance, which involves working out in advance exactly what you want from an audience, then going all out to get it. Effectively the performer is telling the audience how it should react. A director like Peter Brook would not want to work with an actress who went through a script calculating what size of laugh to aim for at each gag or with an actor who turned up at the first rehearsal word-perfect. This degree of pre-determination would preclude the kind of interaction modern directors work for between actor and audience. The reaction against the proscenium arch is also part of the movement towards a more reciprocal audience relationship. But it has to be remembered that rehearsal periods were generally much shorter before the last war and that the style in which Coward acted and directed is inseparable from the style in which he wrote and performed his songs. The relationship he wanted with his audience – and which his audience wanted with him – was more like that of intimate revue.

Nevertheless his plays have already become modern classics. George Devine was keen that he should be represented in the repertoire of the Royal Court and *Look After Lulu*, his adaptation of Feydeau's *Occupe toi d'Amélie*, was staged there in 1959 with Vivien Leigh. Then in 1964 he was invited to direct his own *Hay Fever* at the National Theatre with Dame Edith Evans in the part Marie Tempest had created. In the main tradition of the English theatre Coward has an assured place. His style – a style in which playwright and performer are inseparable – has exerted a central influence on our theatrical history. If a family tree were drawn up to represent the heritage of post-war drama, Wilde and Shaw would have to be shown as ancestors of Coward and Osborne; Pinter and Orton would be among his descendants. In the evolution of English acting the Coward influence can be pinpointed most clearly, of course, in Gielgud, who now occupies a far more central position in the tradition than Coward himself. Just as Gielgud made his Congreve and his Wilde all the funnier by introducing moments of Hamlet-like gravity, he made his Shakespearean tragedy all the more human and moving by importing a lightness of touch which he owed more to Noël Coward than to anyone else.

LAURENCE OLIVIER

❦

'Mr Olivier was about twenty times as much in love with Juliet as Mr Gielgud is, but Mr Giegud speaks most of the poetry far better than Mr Olivier.' This was Herbert Farjeon's judgment in 1935 when Gielgud directed, first playing Mercutio to Olivier's Romeo and, later exchanging parts with him. The rivalry between them was to last for twenty-five years and critics were incessantly comparing them, championing one against the other as the greater actor. In his first book *He that Plays the King* Kenneth Tynan contrasted them in terms of Burke's *Enquiry into the Nature of Ideas upon the Sublime and the Beautiful*, equating Gielgud with the Beautiful and Olivier with the Sublime. He also wrote 'One thinks of Olivier in terms of other species, of panthers and lions: one thinks of Gielgud in terms of other arts, of ballet and portrait painting'. The contrast between them, he said, could be equated with the contrast Dr Johnson had drawn between Milton's ability to carve a colossus out of granite and his inability to carve heads on cherry-stones. 'For the large, shattering effects of passion, we look to Olivier; for the smaller, more exquisite effects of temper, to Gielgud.'

But can it be said that either of the two actors had any influence, positive or negative, on the other? Olivier is three years younger than Gielgud and had only seen a few of his Shakespeare performances by the time they first worked together. Olivier, who was then twenty-eight, was not so much in danger of imitating Gielgud as of recoiling to the opposite extreme, going with all the more vigour and determination for the physical and earthly qualities. 'I'd found that John had got a preoccupation with the beautiful and the poetic, in those days, at the expense of reality. This is certainly, has always been and probably always will be a valid way of approaching Shakespeare. But I've always been much more fascinated by the idea of convincing people that something was *real*. It took me some years to understand this. You certainly can't arrive at it by discarding the Shakespeare and pretending it's prose. You have to achieve reality *through* the verse and not in spite of it – and not leaning entirely upon it either, I would say. It's just the structure of the building and you've got to live in it. But what comes out could seem and be real along the line of moments of recognition: "I see exactly what he's feeling now". I think you'd probably find that that kind of conviction is obscured by what one might call an ultra-lyrical rendition of verse, in which case it's become nearer song than speech. And I've thought that John was drifting away from the sort of reality I remember feeling that he had when he started playing Shakespeare. He spoke Shakespeare as if it was his natural way of speaking when he was young. When he played Hamlet the second time in 1933, he certainly spoke it like his mother tongue. He meant every word he said. But by the time we did *Romeo and Juliet* he seemed to me to be a little conscious of his gifts, of music and lyricism. I think he was going through a stage of being aware of what was expected of him.'

Of course the contrast between their two approaches can easily be overstressed. 'I don't turn my back on lyricism myself and he can be perfectly real when he wants to be.' But the fact that Gielgud's approach to Shakespearean verse was having such a strong tidal pull not only on the other actors in the *Romeo* company but on the profession as a whole made Olivier strike out in the opposite direction. 'It made me sort of rebellious. It made me think that Shakespeare was now being handled in a certain way and because of the extremely strong influence that any man of John's power and gifts would have, all the company would be going that way, so that when I entered this company, I rather cut across it, thinking in my innocence that they'd say "Ah, this is the real one". But of course it never works like that. I wasn't deliberately trying to scupper the fleet. I was trying to make a success, but I was certainly trying to make it in my own way. I think John, in a way, secretly perhaps, rather leant towards my sort of naturalism. But it didn't alter his own convictions about it at all. In fact I saw him going a little further into the expected field of florid elocutory renditions when he was playing Mercutio after he'd started to rehearse Romeo. By that time he had settled for *almost* singing it – which I didn't like. As soon as I see someone acting in Shakespeare and singing with a tremulo in his voice, I just want to go out, because he's not trying to persuade me that anything real is going on at all. He's just saying "Listen to my beautiful voice" and "Do listen to this glorious cadence I'm about to give you now".'

If Gielgud was then going through a phase of vocal self-indulgence he did not stay in it for long. 'It must have been awfully hard for him, having developed that propensity, to come off it, but he did, and does when he feels the need to. I suppose that the time when people are best is when everything that they are works *for* them – when even their faults are right in a part.'

The pendulum has now swung to the opposite extreme: the verse in Shakespeare is more likely to be ignored than over-stressed. Not that greater realism necessarily brings greater reality. 'Realism can be as phoney as anything, anyhow, just as phoney as the most rhodomontadey sort of declamation imaginable. There's a ham natural as well as a ham fat in the other way.'

Actors in the *Romeo and Juliet* company responded warmly to the unaccustomed realism that Olivier introduced but many of the critics were far more hostile than Herbert Farjeon. 'I felt so badly about the flop I made. I remember the next night going to Bronson Albery, the manager, and saying "I'll resign tonight if you like". I got the most terrible notices. I think there was right and wrong on both sides. People I call the honest critics among one's colleagues were I think impressed with the reality I had got into it, and the relationship reality, the absolute physical reality between Juliet and myself for instance, and my physical relations with everybody on the stage. It was generously, sweetly and lauditorily remarked on by one or two people. I remember Guthrie wrote to me about it and he said "I think the critics were right to fault you for your verse-speaking. It isn't very good, you know". I think I learned a little bit during that. It was so funny because a season at the Old Vic followed fairly hard upon that, at the end of which I was referred to as a Shakespearean actor.'

Some of his finest performances have been in Shakespearean parts. When he played Hamlet at the Old Vic in 1937 he again

got into trouble with the verse. 'Mr Olivier does not speak
verse badly,' James Agate remonstrated. 'He does not speak it
at all.' But his voice, his energy and his exciting way of using
his body on stage won high praise. He showed his versatility
and his capacity for self-disguise by following Hamlet with Sir
Toby Belch. He gave a broad extrovert performance and in his
next Old Vic role, Henry V, withdrew ascetically into quiet
military virtues. His first Macbeth completed his first year at
the Old Vic and then in 1938, as Iago, he used the idea of a
homosexual attraction to Othello. His Coriolanus (1938) added
considerably to his reputation as an actor in the heroic tradition, but it was not until the 1944 season at the Old Vic, when
he first played Richard III, that he became a star of the
greatest magnitude. In an interview with Kenneth Tynan he
has said 'There is a phrase – the sweet smell of success – and I
can only tell you (I've had two experiences of that), it just
smells like Brighton and oyster-bars and things like that. And
as I went on to the stage – the house was not even full – I felt
this thing. I felt a little power of hypnotism; I felt that I had
them. It went to my head, as I said, to such an extent that I
didn't even bother to put on the limp. I thought, I've got them
anyway, I needn't bother with all this characterization any
more.' In 1945 at the Vic his famous stammering Hotspur was
followed, in *Part Two* of *Henry IV* by a beautifully contrasted
study in doddering senility as Shallow. He played Lear in 1946,
Antony in 1951, Titus Andronicus and Malvolio at Stratford-
on-Avon in 1955, Othello in 1964 and Shylock in 1970.

His versatility outside the Shakespearean canon has been
equally admirable. He was the original Stanhope in the Stage
Society's production of *Journey's End* and the original Victor
in Coward's *Private Lives*. He played Sergius in *Arms and the
Man* at the Old Vic and in one famous double bill there he un-
forgettably doubled Sophocles's Oedipus with Mr Puff in
Sheridan's *The Critic*. He played the Duke in Fry's *Venus
Observed* and Fred Midway with a Birmingham accent in
David Turner's *Semi-Detached*. Without knowing that all
three were Laurence Olivier it would have been hard to recog-
nize the same actor in Osborne's Archie Rice, Congreve's
Tattle in *Love for Love* and the Jewish lawyer in Somerset
Maugham's *Home and Beauty*.

'I don't know if one does understand one's range. One thing

I'm certain of is that it narrows off as one gets older. There's one thing that dictates that and that's the age itself. When you're a useful age, say between thirty and thirty-five, you can still play Romeo, and you can also play King Lear. Your range is that big because those are the sort of things you can do. But when you get to be King Lear's age, how many ways are there that you can do it? Your way of playing a sixty-five, seventy year old man, your field, has narrowed down to that anyway. Yes, you can find different sorts of men of sixty. The doctor I've just done in *Three Sisters* I hope is unrecognizable from the Captain in *The Dance of Death*. But you very seldom get such widely different sorts of people after a certain age.

What about the solicitor in Somerset Maugham?

'That's a bit of pantomime there. You couldn't do that in a very big part, and keep it clear of everything else. That's taking advantage of a minor role in order to make a small creation, which you can just hold watertight for that amount of time, but if that were stretched over a whole evening, they'd be bound to see bits of Archie Rice come into it, and bits of this and bits of that. You know you can't do it. One started one's life fairly gallantly in rep thinking "Nobody's going to recognize me this week from the people who saw me last week". But as you get older, the things you discover become the things which adhere to you. You say "I wish to God I hadn't done that trick of blinking my eyes in the last part I played because it would be so much more useful this week, and much truer to the character than the one I played last week".

'You can see people doing just the same things, using everything they've got. I remember when I was directing Colin Blakeley in Miller's *The Crucible*, which was soon after he'd played Philoctetes, and I kept saying "Colin don't limp". But having limped through a part successfully like that, suddenly it doesn't feel real if you don't do that. It's a refuge. A mannerism is something you develop in order to make you feel more comfortable. And if one day you're terribly nervous on a first night, someone says "The carriage waits, my lord. My Lord Pilkington – " and if one day you come on and go like that (tucking his chin into his shoulder and lumbering one-sidedly) because you're shy of the audience or something – if you don't know it, you're stuck with that for life. Because you

cannot bear the thought of not having one little refuge, something you're used to – a habit – something to make you comfortable. When we go to bed we usually get into the same
position, foetal or not – it's comfort. Therefore when you
come on the stage and you think "Oh God, I hope I don't get
the wind up, Oh God I hope I've got this, Oh God I hope I
remember that", and then you do that (going into the same
position) that's at least home for a minute, a second. Your
anxiety is to feel at home if you're up in an awkward draughty
position like you are on a stage in front of a lot of people –
therefore for John Gielgud a certain tone of voice is home.
You lean on those, find refuge in those things, they're terribly
seductive. So that a thing you've done before feels real because you're used to it – you don't realize that at the time. It's
impossible to go on stretching yourself into being different
shapes and sizes, particularly as your age is governing the main
factor which is stopping you playing Romeo at least. You
don't do that. You can't even play Mercutio. I was a bit old
for the Captain in *The Dance of Death* really. You're supposed
to be fifty. I suppose I'm fairly young for my age. My way
of carrying on is fairly young – I realize that. I've kept very
fit and very physical and all that. But there are a lot of things
that one does with one's body that one does unknowingly in
the search for a refuge.'

A habit that has helped him to develop and sustain his protean
range is his way of concentrating on physical details, whether
of costume or make-up, accent or prop, in the process of
adapting to them. Ronald Pickup, who has spent most of his
career in the National company, has gained a lot from watching Olivier. 'What I've learnt from him is always to deal in
specific very concrete intentions, never in generalizations. You
have to know exactly why you're doing and saying anything at
any moment. That's what creates a faster rhythm. He took such
pains that his watch-strap was right in O'Neill's *Long Day's
Journey*, and he wore his suit for three or four weeks before
we opened. He asked me the other day what sort of walk I'd
got for Richard II. I hadn't actually got a walk at that time
but it made me think about that and about other things
related to it. It's getting a comfortable physical sensation for

the character and knowing that everything about you feels right. Everything then becomes effortless. The intentions take over and you start to fly. What I've learnt about Olivier – which is not the most readily apparent thing – is the dazzling speed at which his thinking happens in terms of the character, this marvellous driving rhythm, the ability to be operating on about eight different levels at once, always keeping an audience on the hop, never letting them get ahead. It really boils down to rhythm. The pulse-beat of anything is what drives it along, and the faster your rhythm is, the more exciting you're likely to be.'

This view of his powers as an actor is confirmed and complemented by Albert Finney's experience of understudying his Coriolanus. 'What one did learn from that is how a great actor can take the kind of peaks and the valleys of a performance, the ups and downs of a character as written and push them even further apart. He makes the climaxes higher, and he makes the depths of it lower, than you feel is possible in the text.'

While John Gielgud keeps his mind alert and derives a good deal of his inspiration from reading and looking at pictures in galleries, Olivier seems to draw more on physical experience. 'I learnt a lot about a very essential factor in acting – poise, the feeling of poise – from flying an aeroplane. It was very interesting, because your two enemies are tautness and ultra-relaxation, in anything you're trying to do, if it's cricket or any physical thing. And acting is largely a physical thing – it's to do with the senses of all sorts. It's the same equation you've got to find between tautness or over-relaxation, or between under-confidence or over-confidence. It's very difficult to find just the right amount. The difficulty of acting, I've always thought, is finding the right humility towards the work and the right confidence to carry it out. With flying you have to learn at least a very exact, precise poise, between your feet being too heavy on the rudder, or your hand too heavy on the stick or too savage on the throttle. You learn a kind of very special poise. And that I've managed to bring into the acting – frightfully useful. Or managed to remember it when I needed to. "Now wait a miute, you're taut". Or "You're too relaxed". It's come in very useful.'

It cannot be said that his relationship with Iago came off

well in the National Theatre *Othello*, but his ideas about it derived partly from wartime experience. 'Rather in common with most people I've come to look on the NCO Iago as the right one, because from my own experience in the war, I've known what an Iago felt like. I've seen people's expressions in the mess or the ward room or whatever you call it, when somebody suddenly gets a half stripe that they'd thought was going to be theirs. I've been conscious of situations in the service myself when with certain groups of men in certain ranks, you find things in yourself that you didn't know were there in the way of jealousies and sensitivities and bloody-mindedness and hatred. And you could be guilty of Iago's offence with the greatest of ease, if you hadn't had just enough sense. I've wanted to kill men, I've wanted to do people down very much when I was in the service, and I think in every service they know that. It's a difficult life. I found the so-called ordinary people so terribly ordinary, so lacking in imagination, I'd hate them for it. They didn't understand each other's feelings at all. I thought when I joined "How marvellous, now I shall know real people, instead of this froth that I've been living amongst all my life". My God, give me the froth every time for real people. Real people are artists. Ordinary people aren't. They just exist in a kind of vacuum. Without any pity, feeling, imagination about each other's troubles or woes or sensitivities or sensibilities. Almost inhuman, I found the real people.'

The frustration Olivier feels at the diminution of range that age brings must have been compensated at least by the satisfactions of directing both in the theatre and the cinema, and of managing, first in the commercial theatre, then at Chichester and the National. His company, Laurence Olivier Productions Limited, presented several plays in the West End, and in 1950, after five years as a Joint Artistic Director of the Old Vic, he leased the St James's Theatre which he kept until 1956, the year before it was closed down. Apart from the plays in which he and his wife Vivien Leigh starred, he presented Dennis Cannan's *Captain Carvallo*, the Orson Welles *Othello* and Tyrone Guthrie's play *Top of the Ladder*, but he also had to sub-let the theatre for long periods. His association with Guthrie, which had begun at the Old Vic, was to culminate in the planning of the Chichester Festival Theatre. Its design was inspired by Guthrie; Olivier was Artistic

Director for its first four seasons; Guthrie had encouraged
Leslie Evershed Martin in the formidable task of raising the
money and bringing the theatre into existence. So Olivier's assumption of the artistic crown when our National Theatre
opened in 1963 was the culmination of a long career in theatrical management. Of course the strain of running a large company as well as acting and directing was enormous. 'The thing
that tires you most and quickest is the thing you resist first.
And of course that's the acting. With all that I've got to do
today and a performance tonight, I think that would make me
feel tomorrow "I don't think I can manage". With *Othello* for
instance, I really felt all the next day I was useless in the office
– as if I had been run over by a bus.'

Olivier's orientation has always been primarily towards the
theatre, but he has also devoted a considerable proportion of
his career to the cinema. He spent 1938-40 in Hollywood and
he has appeared in over forty films, as well as directing six.
His work as a film director has been strongly influenced by the
feeling for rhythm and for shape that he had acquired in the
theatre. His three Shakespeare films, *Henry V, Hamlet* and
Richard III undoubtedly won a wider audience for Shakespeare than he had ever had before – even in the cinema – but
Olivier has had to make cuts that he very much regretted. 'I
had to tear my heart out by cutting "All occasions" in *Hamlet*,
which to me is of course the most important speech of the
play. But you have to cut it, because it was just dangerous to
get discursive there, from a film put-together point of view.
Because of the solid impact the medium needs, it has to exist
in a certain form – there are a variety of forms of course. It's
just that certain things are dangerous in certain ways, on certain subjects, in certain conditions, and you probably don't
really know until you see the rushes.' In *Richard III* he had
to cut heavily into Clarence's scene. 'It's a long scene. Nothing's
long, as long as it doesn't seem long but the early part of the
picture seemed a long time getting going. And there are some
points in a film – rhythm of course is the chief of all our
studies – when you just know it's dangerous to get discursive.'

He also had complicated problems of shape and rhythm in
the film he made of Chekhov's *Three Sisters*, though it was an
advantage, of course, to have become so familiar with the play
from directing it in the theatre. 'I've always known the

dangerous moments in it. The danger is the second act of the four. Not the third, which everybody thinks is the dangerous one – the first scene, when everybody is so lazy they can do nothing but sit about. That holds together like a glove.' He was determined to make the film very much more than a cinematic record of his National Theatre production, though he used many of the same actors in the same parts. 'It's a proper film, but you don't go outside and have scenes of people fire-fighting – that's so boring and you can't, there isn't time. Whenever I did get at all discursive, I found that the film people, who were my advisors, and in some sense I suppose my bosses, the Boulting brothers and Sidney Gilliat of British Lion – all they wanted to cut were the bits I put in to make it more like a film, to get out of that room, to create a little scene, down a staircase or in another room. They said "That holds up the action. Get back to it", and I said "Now you're forcing me back onto the stage again". But the only thing I did try to lend myself to was more filmic ideas of setting and getting a little out of the usual way of thinking about that play.'

Though there was a great deal that he liked about Sidney Lumet's film of Chekhov's *The Seagull*, the main influence that it exerted on him was negative. 'It looked marvellous sometimes. There is the occasional pure Monet, for instance, in that shot with Vanessa on the left in full figure, with the lake and rushes behind, looking at him, the first time she fell in love with him. A lot of it was very good. But I was grateful to it because it drove me away from reality for my own film because I thought "You couldn't have had more help from reality, realism, real trees". But I don't actually believe they help Chekhov. All I think you can do is to serve the author rhythmically. And all I said to Josef Svoboda, who designed *Three Sisters,* was "Look, I don't care how you do it, I'm having one interval and I will give you one minute to change from the bedroom (Act Three) to the garden (Act Four), one minute. Now do anything you like". And the change took one minute fifty seconds. That's the thing to do for Chekhov – one interval, no more. By the time they've gone out for their third whisky, they say "What's happened now? Where are we? Did they get to Moscow?" You've let Chekhov kill himself with those three intervals. It's so palpably right to go straight from Act One to Act Two of *Uncle Vanya*, straight from Act Three to Act Four. Because of the rhythm. It was that alone that made the productions perhaps better than they've often been. It made all the difference to the audience's attention and participation. It was simply that they were allowed to stay there. All right you give them half a minute, while they breathe or you play something to make a light change happen or something, and they're still there instead of all this business of "What's this? Did you see . . .?" All that bar-room conversation, it's fatal.'

ACKNOWLEDGMENTS

Six of the interviews on which these chapters are based were originally done for *The Times*, and shorter versions of them appeared on the Arts Page. I am grateful to the Editor for permission to incorporate this material and I should also like to express thanks to John Higgins, the Arts Editor, who commissioned me to do them in the first place.

The interview with David Storey was done for *Drama*, and I am grateful to its Executive Editor, Walter Lucas, both for commissioning it and allowing me to use it again. Part of the Scofield interview appeared in *Theatre* 71 edited by Sheridan Morley and published by Hutchinson, so I am also thankful to them for permission to use this material. The interviews with Sir Noël Coward and Lord Olivier have not appeared in any other form.

Obviously I am grateful to all my subjects for giving me the interviews and I am especially indebted to those who have taken additional time to help me in preparing their section of this book.

Finally, I should like to thank Christine Bernard, whose editorial help has been invaluable.

aRoss
—